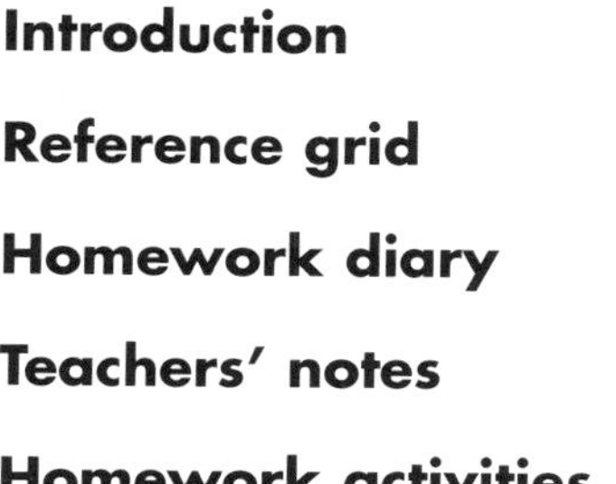

Published by
Scholastic Ltd,
Villiers House,
Clarendon Avenue,
Leamington Spa,
Warwickshire CV32 5PR

Printed by Ebenezer Baylis and Son Ltd, Worcester

1 2 3 4 5 6 7 8 9 0   2 3 4 5 6 7 8 9 0 1

Authors
Carole Creary and Gay Wilson

Editor
David Sandford

Assistant Editor
Clare Gallaher

Series Designer
Micky Pledge

Designers
Micky Pledge, Rachel Warner

Cover photography
Martyn Chillmaid/Photodisc

Illustrations
Jenny Tulip

Acknowledgments
The National Curriculum for England 2000
© The Queens Printer and Controller of HMSO. Reproduced under the terms of HMSO Guidance Note 8.

A Scheme of Work for Key Stages 1 and 2: Science
© Qualifications and Curriculum Authority. Reproduced under the terms of HMSO Guidance Note 8.

British Library Cataloguing-in-Publication Data
A catalogue record for this book is available from the British Library.

ISBN 0-590-53649-4

Teachers should consult their own school policies and guidelines concerning practical work and participation of children in science experiments. You should only select activities which you feel can be carried out safely and confidently in the classroom.

100 SCIENCE HOMEWORK ACTIVITIES

100 Science Homework Activities is a series of resource books for teachers of Years 1–6 (Scottish Primary 1–7). Each book of 100 activiiies covers two year groups, with around 50 activities specific to each year. These provide a 'core' of homework tasks in line with the National Curriculum documents for science in England, Wales and Northern Ireland and, in England, the QCA's *Science Scheme of Work.* The tasks also meet the requirements of the 5–14 National Guidelines for science in Scotland.

The homework activities are intended as a support for all science teachers, be they school science leader or trainee teacher. They can be used with any science scheme of work as the basis for planning homework activities throughout the school in line with your homework policy. If you are using the companion series, *100 Science Lessons*, these books are designed to complement the lesson plans in the corresponding year's book. Activities can be used with single- or mixed-age classes, single- and mixed-ability groups, and for team planning of homework across a year or key stage. You may also find the activities valuable for extension work in class, or as additional resources.

Using the books

100 Science Homework Activities has been planned to offer a range of simple science exercises for children to carry out at home. Many are designed for sharing with a helper, who could be a parent or carer, another adult in the family, an older sibling, or a neighbour. They include a variety of games, puzzles, observations and practical investigations, each of which has been chosen to ensure complete coverage of all UK national curricula for science.

Teacher support

There are supporting teachers' notes for each of the 100 activities in this book, briefly outlining the following:

Learning objectives: the specific learning objectives that the homework aims to address, based on the four curriculum documents, and linked to the same learning objectives from the relevant *100 Science Lessons* book

Lesson context: a brief description of the classroom experience recommended for the children before undertaking the homework activity

Setting the homework: advice on how to explain the worksheet to the children, and how to set it in context before it is taken home

Back at school: suggestions for how to respond to the completed homework, including discussion with the children or specific advice on marking, as well as answers where relevant.

Photocopiable pages

Each of the 100 homework activities in this book includes a photocopiable worksheet for children to take home. The page provides instructions for the child and a brief explanation of the task for the helper, stating simply and clearly the activity's purpose and suggesting ideas for support or a further challenge to offer the child. The science topic addressed by each activity, and the type of homework being offered, are both indicated at the top of each page. There are seven types of homework activity:

Science to share activities encourage the child, with their helper, to talk and work together on a science task. These tasks draw heavily on things likely to be found at home.

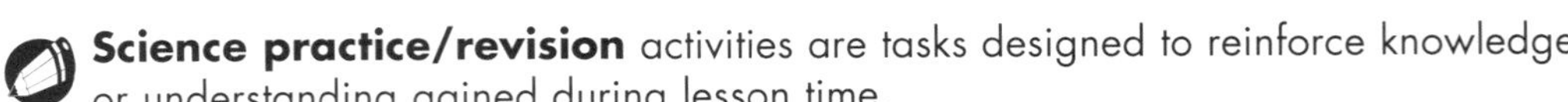
Science practice/revision activities are tasks designed to reinforce knowledge or understanding gained during lesson time.

Numeracy/Literacy link activities practise skills from other areas of the curriculum within a science context.

Finding out activities are designed to increase children's knowledge through investigations, keeping diaries, or by consulting simple secondary sources.

Observation tasks require children to look closely and carefully at things around the home to gain more detailed knowledge of a science topic.

Ask an adult activities help children to understand that asking questions is a valuable way of finding out more about a particular subject, particularly when they are too young to have experienced a particular activity or event themselves.

The grids on pages 4–7 provide an overview of the book's content, showing how each activity can be matched to the curriculum: in England to the National Curriculum for science and the QCA *Science Scheme of Work,* and in Scotland to the 5–14 National Guidelines.

Using these activities with the *100 Science Lessons* series

The organisation of the homework activities in this book matches that of the activities in *100 Science Lessons: Year 1* and *100 Science Lessons: Year 2* (both written by Carole Creary and Gay Wilson, published by Scholastic), so that there are homework activities matching the learning objectives in each unit of work. The grids on pages 4–7 in this book show which lessons in *100 Science Lessons: Year 1* and *Year 2* have associated homework activities here, together with the relevant page numbers from the main books to help with planning.

Supporting your helpers

As well as the notes on each of the worksheets, there is a photocopiable homework diary – provided on page 8 – which can be sent home with each of the homework activities. The diary has space for recording three pieces of homework, and multiple copies can be stapled together to make a longer-term homework record. There is space to record the activity's title and the date it was sent home, and spaces for responses to the homework from the child, the helper and your own comment. The diary is intended to encourage home–school links, so that parents or carers know what is being taught and can make informed comments about their child's progress.

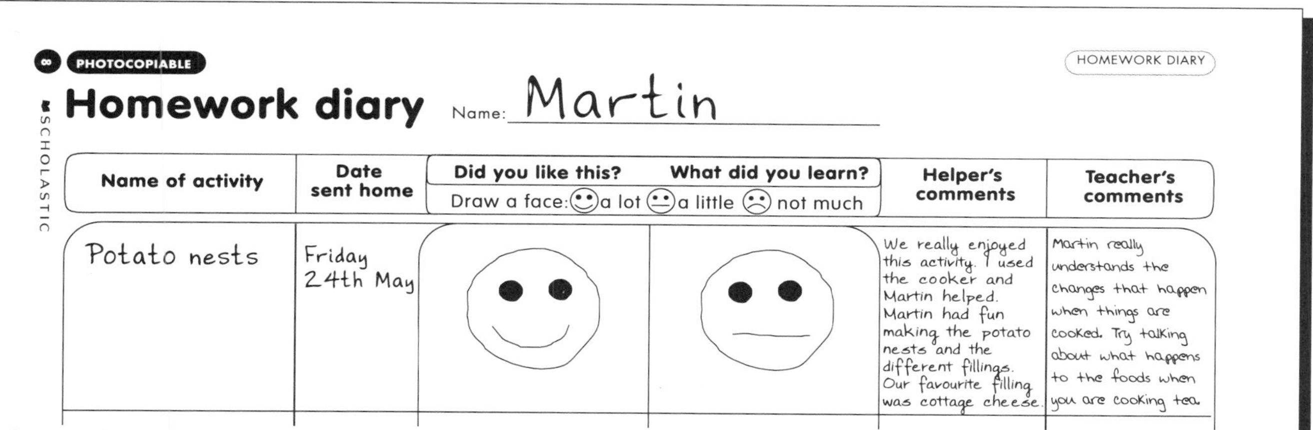

8 PHOTOCOPIABLE — HOMEWORK DIARY — SCHOLASTIC

Homework diary Name: Martin

Name of activity	Date sent home	Did you like this? (Draw a face: a lot / a little / not much)	What did you learn?	Helper's comments	Teacher's comments
Potato nests	Friday 24th May			We really enjoyed this activity. I used the cooker and Martin helped. Martin had fun making the potato nests and the different fillings. Our favourite filling was cottage cheese	Martin really understands the changes that happen when things are cooked. Try talking about what happens to the foods when you are cooking tea.

About this book: Years 1&2/Primary 1–3

This book provides 100 creative science homeworks for six- to seven-year-olds. Each unit offers between three and nine activities to support a topic, so even if you choose not to use all the activities as homework there is plenty of choice, and a wealth of extension material for use in the classroom, particularly with classroom helpers.

For young children, science is all about experience, and beginning to make sense of the world immediately around them. Although the activities have been categorised, almost all the activities in this book could also be labelled 'science to share', since they encourage children to explore science tasks together with a helper. The majority of the activities need no special resources, using only simple household equipment, or things that are commonly available at home. Many encourage the children to make use of their local environment, or to draw on experience of their surroundings, where adult supervision is clearly essential.

All areas of the National Curriculum are covered in this book. Activities on space, energy and electricity at Year 1 have been included to meet Scottish requirements, and to support teachers elsewhere who are not following the QCA *Science Scheme of Work*. Although the activities in both halves of the book cover similar content, those for Year 2/Primary 2–3 build on those for Year 1/Primary 1–2 and are generally more demanding, not only in terms of scientific understanding but also in terms of literacy and numeracy. In Years 1 & 2/Primary 1–3, children will be at many different stages of learning to read and write, so you will need to make it clear to helpers that they should read the instructions with children and, if necessary, help them with their writing.

Page in this book	Activity name	Homework type	Learning objectives	QCA Unit	National Curriculum	Scottish 5–14 Guidelines	Unit	Lesson	Page
29	Getting dressed	Science practice	To know that there are different external parts of the human body	1A	Sc2 2a	The processes of life – A	1	1	12
30	Name the senses	Literacy link	To know about the human senses	1A	Sc2 2a	The processes of life – A	1	3	15
31	Let's go round the mulberry bush	Literacy link	To know that the human body can move in different ways	1A	Sc2 1b	The processes of life – A	1	7	18
32	Me growing up	Numeracy link	To know about how they have grown from birth to present day	1A	Sc2 1b	The processes of life – A	1	8	20
33	My family	Science practice	To know that there are different stages in the human life cycle	1A	Sc2 1b	The processes of life – A	1	9	21
34	Shopping for food and drink	Science to share	To know that food and water are needed for animals, including humans, to stay alive; To carry out a simple survey	1A	Sc2 2b	The processes of life – A; Developing informed attitudes	1	10	23
35	Dead or alive?	Science practice	To know how to distinguish between a living thing and a non-living thing	1B	Sc2 1a	The processes of life – A	2	1	36
36	What is it?	Science practice	To recognise and name some common animals	1B	Sc2 5a	The processes of life – A	2	2	37
37	Beetle	Numeracy link	To recognise and name the main external parts of the bodies of animals	1B	Sc2 2a	The processes of life – A	2	3	39
38	How do they move?	Observation	To know that animals can move in different ways from humans	1B	Sc2 1b	Interaction of living things with their environment – A	2	4	39
39	I-spy plants	Observation	To recognise and name some common plants	1B	Sc2 5a	Variety and characteristic features – A	2	7	42
40	Growing seeds is fun	Finding out	To know that most plants grow from seeds	1B	Sc2 3c	The processes of life – B	2	8	43
41	Sort the tins	Finding out	To know that plants provide a range of foods; To be able to match some foods to their plant of origin	1B	Sc2 2c (3b)	–	2	13	52
42	Salad for tea	Literacy link	To know that some foods are prepared directly from plants	1B	Sc2 2c (3b)	Variety and characteristic features – A	2	14	53
43	Weather record	Numeracy link	To know that there are simple features of the weather that can be observed; To collect data	–	–	On planet Earth – A	3	2	67
44	Blowing in the wind	Finding out	To make and use a simple wind meter to measure the strength and direction of the wind	–	–	On planet Earth – A	3	4	69
45	Signs of the seasons – autumn	Science to share	To know how the environment changes as the year passes through the seasons	–	–	Earth in space – A	3	5	70
46	Signs of the seasons – winter	Observation	To know how the environment changes as the year passes through the seasons	–	–	Earth in space – A	3	6	72
47	Signs of the seasons – spring	Observation	To know how the environment changes as the year passes through the seasons	–	–	Earth in space – A	3	7	72
48	Signs of the seasons – summer	Science practice	To know how the environment changes as the year passes through the seasons	–	–	Earth in space – A	3	8	72
49	I-spy minibeasts	Numeracy link	To know the names of some common animals (minibeasts) in the local environment	–	Sc2 5a	Variety and characteristic features – B	3	10	74
50	Feed the birds	Science to share	To know the names of some common animals (birds) in the local environment	–	Sc2 5a	Variety and characteristic features – B	3	11	76
51	My bedroom	Literacy link	To know that a habitat is a relatively small part of the environment and is the home of a plant or animal	–	Sc2 5b	Variety and characteristic features – A	3	12	77
52	What's it like?	Literacy link	To know that different materials have different properties	1C	Sc3 1a, 1b	Materials from Earth – A	4	1	95
53	What's it made from?	Science practice	To be able to identify some common materials	1C	Sc3 1c	Materials from Earth – A	4	2	97

Page in this book	Activity name	Homework type	Learning objectives	QCA Unit	National Curriculum	Scottish 5–14 Guidelines	Unit	Lesson	Page
54	**Is it magnetic?**	Finding out	To know that some materials are magnetic, but most are not	1C	Sc3 1b	–	4	6	100
55	**More of the same**	Numeracy link	To know that a range of materials are used in our environment; To know that materials can be used in a variety of ways	1C	Sc3 1d	Materials from Earth – B	4	9	102
56	**How many things?**	Science practice	To know that different objects can be made from the same material	1C	Sc3 1d	Materials from Earth – A	4	10	104
57	**How many materials?**	Literacy link	To know that an object can be made of several materials	1C	Sc3 1d	Materials from Earth – A	4	11	105
58	**Is it waterproof?**	Science to share	To carry out a simple investigation with help; To know that some materials are waterproof and others are not	1C	Sc1 2a 2b	Materials from Earth – B	4	12	107
59	**Egg sandwiches**	Literacy link	To know that some materials are changed in shape by forces	1C	Sc3 2a	–	4	13	109
60	**Electrical things**	Science practice	To know that many appliances need electricity to make them work	–	Sc4 1a	–	5	1	122
61	**Batteries**	Science practice	To know that electricity is obtained from the mains or from batteries (cells)	–	Sc4 1a	–	5	2	124
62	**Electricity Snakes and Ladders**	Science to share	To know that electricity can be dangerous and must be treated with extreme care	1E	Sc4 1a	Properties and uses of energy – A; Developing informed attitudes	5	3	126
63	**Me moving**	Science practice	To know that there are different kinds of movement	1E	Sc4 2b,c	Forces and their effects – A	6	1	138
64	**Using forces to move things**	Science practice	To know that forces can move objects and change their direction; To begin to understand cause and effect	1E	Sc4 2b, c	Forces and their effects – B	6	3	141
65	**Using forces to change a shape**	Science practice	To know that forces such as pushes, pulls and twists can change an object's shape	1E	Sc3 2a	Forces and their effects – B	6	4	143
66	**Blow football**	Science to share	To consider the wind as a force; To know that wind is moving air; To know that the wind can make things move	1E	Sc4 2a	Forces and their effects – B; On planet Earth – A	6	6	145
67	**Pushing down and pushing up**	Finding out	To experience the upward push (force) of water; To know that water pushes upwards on objects	1E	Sc4 2a	Forces and their effects – A	6	8	147
68	**In the dark**	Finding out	To know that light is needed for us to see things	1D	Sc4 3b	Forms and sources of energy – A	7	1	154
69	**Light**	Numeracy link	To know that there are many sources of light	1D	Sc4 3a	Forms and sources of energy – A	7	2	155
70	**Very bright**	Literacy link	To know that light sources can vary in brightness	1D	Sc4 3a	Forms and sources of energy – A	7	3	157
71	**In an emergency**	Science practice	To know how to call the emergency services	1F	Sc4 4c	Developing informed attitudes	7	6	161
72	**Sounds at home**	Science practice	To know that there are many different sources of sound in the locality	1F	Sc4 4c	Forms and sources of energy – A; Properties and uses of energy – A	7	8	163
73	**Making music**	Science to share	To identify some objects that make sounds	1F	Sc4 4c	Forms and sources of energy – A; Properties and uses of energy – A	7	9	163
74	**Nasty noises**	Science practice	To know that a 'noise' is often an unpleasant sound; To know that loud noises can be harmful	1F	Sc4 4c	Properties and uses of energy – A	7	13	167
75	**Helpful sounds**	Literacy link	To know that our hearing helps to keep us safe	1F	Sc2 2g	Developing informed attitudes	7	18	174
76	**Moon watch**	Literacy link	To know that the Moon is a sphere; To know that the Moon appears to change its shape	–	–	Earth in space – A	8	2	184
77	**Sun, Moon and stars**	Science practice	To distinguish the Sun and the Moon from the stars	–	–	Earth in space – A	8	3	187
78	**Night work**	Finding out	To know that the pattern of day and night affects animals	–	–	Earth in space – A	8	4	187

YEAR 2 REFERENCE GRID

Page in this book	Activity name	Homework type	Learning objectives	QCA Unit	National Curriculum	Scottish 5–14 Guidelines	Unit	Lesson	Page
79	Food groups	Science practice	To know that food can be put into groups; To know that knowledge of food groups can help us build healthy diets	2A, 2C	Sc2 1b, 2b, 2c	The processes of life – A; Respect and care for self and others	1	1	13
80	Exercise diary	Literacy link	To know that regular exercise is needed to maintain good health	2A, 2C	Sc2 2c	The processes of life – A; Respect and care for self and others	1	4	16
81	Sleep diary	Numeracy link	To know that enough and regular sleep is needed for good health	2A, 2C	Sc2 2c	The processes of life – A; Respect and care for self and others	1	5	18
82	Cleaning teeth	Science to share	To know that the mouth needs care and attention to keep it healthy	2A, 2C	Sc2 1b	The processes of life – A; Respect and care for self and others	1	6	18
83	Bath time	Science to share	To know that the skin needs to be kept clean for good health	2A, 2C	Sc2 2c	The processes of life – A; Respect and care for self and others	1	7	20
84	People who care	Finding out	To know that young humans need care while they are growing up	2A, 2C	Sc2 2f	The processes of life – B	1	13	29
85	How we change	Ask an adult	To know that our appearance changes over time	2A, 2C	Sc2 2f	The processes of life – B	1	16	31
86	Plant or animal?	Science practice	To know the difference between an animal and a plant	2B, 2C	Sc2 4b	Variety and characteristic features – A	2	1	46
87	Animal or plant?	Science practice	To sort a group of living things into animals or plants	2B, 2C	Sc2 4b	Variety and characteristic features – A	2	3	49
88	My plant	Literacy link	To know how to use secondary sources to find out about plants	2B, 2C	Sc2 5a	Processes of life – B; Interaction of living things with their environment – A	2	6	52
89	At the supermarket	Science to share	To know that there are many different types of fruits and seeds	2B, 2C	Sc2 3c	Processes of life – B	2	8	54
90	Seedy?	Science to share	To know that different fruits contain different numbers of seeds	2B, 2C	Sc2 3c	Processes of life – B	2	9	54
91	Animal groups	Science practice	To know that animals can be sorted into groups	2B, 2C	Sc2 4b	Variety and characteristic features – B; Processes of life – B	2	12	57
92	Native animals	Literacy link	To know how to use secondary sources to find out about a wide range of animals	2B, 2C	Sc2 5a	Variety and characteristic features – B; Processes of life – B; Interaction of living things with their environment – A	2	13	59
93	Butterfly changes	Finding out	To know that animals reproduce and change as they grow older	2B, 2C	Sc2 2f	Processes of life – B	2	15	60
94	I-spy plants and animals	Observation	To know the names of some of the plants and animals in the local environment	2B	Sc2 5a	Interaction of living things with their environment – A	3	1	73
95	Comparing plants	Observation	To know that plants in the local environment are similar to each other in some ways and different in others	2B	Sc2 5b	Interaction of living things with their environment – A	3	4	76
96	Seashore	Finding out	To know some of the plants and animals in a named habitat	2B	Sc2 5a	Interaction of living things with their environment – A	3	5	78
97	Who needs what?	Science to share	To know that living things in a habitat depend on each other	2B	Sc2 5a	Interaction of living things with their environment – A	3	8	80
98	Seasonal change	Science practice	To know that plants and animals change in appearance and behaviour with the seasons	2B	Sc2 5a	Interaction of living things with their environment – A	3	11	83
99	In my street	Science to share	To know ways in which the environment can be cared for	2B	Sc2 5c	Interaction of living things with their environment – A; Respect and care for others	3	12	85
100	Look for labels	Finding out	To know that fabrics are made from different materials	2D	Sc3 1a, b, c	Materials from Earth – A	4	2	97
101	Useful materials	Science practice	To know about everyday uses of some materials	2D	Sc3 1d	Materials from Earth – A	4	3	97
102	Natural materials	Literacy link	To know that some materials occur naturally	2D	Sc3 1c	Materials from Earth – A	4	4	99
103	It's not natural	Science to share	To know that some materials are not natural but are manufactured	2D	Sc3 1c	Materials from Earth – A	4	5	101

Page in this book	Activity name	Homework type	Learning objectives	QCA Unit	National Curriculum	Scottish 5–14 Guidelines	Unit	Lesson	Page
104	**Potato nests**	Science to share	To know that materials often change when they are heated	2D	Sc3 2b	Changing Materials – B	4	7	105
105	**Look for steam**	Finding out	To know that water turns to steam when it is heated, but the steam turns back to water when it is cooled	2D	Sc3 2b	Changing Materials – B	4	9	107
106	**Cool it!**	Science to share	To know that some materials change when they are cooled	2D	Sc3 2b	Changing Materials – B	4	10	108
107	**Cheese on toast**	Observation	To know that some materials melt and change when they are heated	2D	Sc3 2a	Changing Materials – A	4	11	109
108	**Hot spots**	Finding out	To know that heat is a form of energy and that it may be supplied by several sources.	2D	Sc3 2b	Changing Materials – B; Social and environmental responsibility	4	13	112
109	**How many ways?**	Finding out	To know that electricity is used in many different ways; To know that mains electricity can be very dangerous	2F	Sc4 1a	Properties and uses of energy – A; Respect and care for self and others	5	1	124
110	**Safety first**	Science practice	To know that mains electricity can be very dangerous and must be treated with extreme care	2F	Sc4 1a	Properties and uses of energy – A; Respect and care for self and others	5	2	125
111	**What uses batteries?**	Science to share	To know that electricity can be supplied by batteries (cells)	2F	Sc4 1b	Properties and uses of energy – A	5	3	126
112	**Complete the circuit**	Science practice	To know that a complete circuit is needed for a device to work; To know the names of the components needed for a circuit to make a bulb light	2F	Sc4 1b	Properties and uses of energy – A; Conversion and transfer of energy – B	5	4	127
113	**Pull or push?**	Science practice	To know that forces make things move	2E	Sc4 2a	Forces and their effects – A	6	1	138
114	**Push, pull or twist?**	Science practice	To know that actions such as stretching, squeezing, squashing, twisting and turning can be explained as forces	2E	Sc4 2b	Forces and their effects – A, B	6	2	140
115	**Forces wordsearch**	Literacy link	To know that there is a force of friction between two surfaces	2E	Sc4 2b, c	Forces and their effects – A, B	6	3	141
116	**Speeding up, slowing down**	Observation	To know that forces can make moving objects go faster, change direction or slow down	2E	Sc4 2c	Forces and their effects – A, B	6	6	144
117	**Sinking bottles**	Numeracy link	To know that some objects float because water pushes up on them	2E	Sc4 2b	Forces and their effects – A, B	6	10	148
118	**All lit up**	Science practice	To know that light sources are used in different ways	–	Sc4 3a	Properties and use of energy – A, B	7	1	157
119	**Shadows**	Science to share	To know that light cannot pass through some materials and that is how shadows are created	–	Sc4 3b	Properties and use of energy – B	7	2	159
120	**Transparent, translucent, opaque**	Science practice	To know that light can pass through some materials, but not others	–	Sc4 3b	Properties and use of energy – B	7	4	161
121	**Solar energy**	Finding out	To know that light is a form of energy	–	Sc4 3b	Properties and use of energy – B	7	5	163
122	**Sounds at home**	Literacy link	To know that we make use of sounds in a variety of ways	–	Sc4 4c	Properties and use of energy – A	7	6	165
123	**Warning sounds**	Observation	To know that sounds can act as warnings	–	Sc4 4c	Properties and use of energy – A	7	7	167
124	**Making sounds**	Science to share	To know how to make a range of sounds using a collection of materials and objects	–	Sc4 4c	Properties and use of energy – A, B	7	8	167
125	**Sound puzzle**	Literacy link	To know that sounds get fainter as they travel away from a source and that loud sounds travel further than quiet sounds	–	Sc4 4d	Properties and use of energy – A, B	7	11	171
126	**Sun diary**	Finding out	To know that the Sun appears to move across the sky in a regular way	–	Sc4 3a	Earth and space – A, B	8	1	183
127	**The Moon in space**	Literacy link	To know that we only see the Moon because it reflects light from the Sun	–	Sc4 3a	Earth and space – A	8	4	187
128	**Mapping the weather**	Science to share	To use weather records to see the pattern of the seasons	–	–	Earth and space – B	8	5	189

Homework diary

Name: ______________________

Name of activity	Date sent home	Did you like this?	What did you learn?	Helper's comments	Teacher's comments
		Draw a face: a lot, a little, not much			

TEACHERS' NOTES

UNIT 1 OURSELVES ME AND MY BODY

P29 Getting dressed — SCIENCE PRACTICE

Learning objective

- To know that there are different external parts of the human body.

Lesson context

Help the children to learn the names and positions of familiar and less familiar body parts. Discuss how we all have the same body parts in the same places and yet we all look different.

Setting the homework

Hold up a coat or jumper and ask the children to tell you which of their body parts is covered by the garment. Ask them to complete the labels on the homework sheet by writing the names of the correct body parts in the spaces.

Back at school

Ask a child to come to the front of the class. Can the other children name the body parts covered by the child's visible clothes?

p30 Name the senses — LITERACY LINK

Learning objective

- To know about the human senses.

Lesson context

Using role-play, let the children practise identifying the senses that are used in different scenarios, for example smelling something burning. Encourage them to develop language that enables them to describe their observations. They should be able to name the five senses and to discuss how each is useful.

Setting the homework

Make sure that the children can identify what is happening in each picture. Tell them that their task is to use the words at the bottom of the page to complete the label for each picture. This will reinforce vocabulary.

Back at school

Gather the children together and, using a spare copy of the worksheet, ask them to tell you which sense goes with which picture. Finish off by saying, 'We hear with our ears' together, and asking them to point to the relevant parts of their bodies.

p31 Let's go round the mulberry bush — LITERACY LINK

Learning objective

- To know that the human body can move in a variety of different ways.

Lesson context

Look at a model or picture of a human skeleton with the children and identify some of the joints, then ask them to find the same joint on their own bodies. During play activities, see if they can identify which joints they are using. Talk about the different types of joint and how they move.

Setting the homework

This activity reinforces the children's vocabulary and ideas about joints and movement. Make sure that they know the tune to 'Here we go round the mulberry bush' and are familiar with the game. Tell the children they are going to play this game with their helper.

Back at school

Play the game again. Invite children to contribute some new actions, and to identify the joints being used.

p32 Me growing up — NUMERACY LINK

Learning objective

- To know about how they have grown from birth to the present day.

Lesson context

Discuss how the children have changed from birth to the present day, including physical changes and capabilities. If possible, have a parent and baby visit the class and talk about the differences between the baby and themselves. Discuss their increasing independence as they grow older.

Setting the homework

Developing sequencing and ordering skills is a key prerequisite of accurate counting. Tell the children that they should complete the worksheet with pictures of themselves as they have grown up from being a baby. Make sure they understand that sticking photographs to the sheet is not necessary, and that they can draw pictures instead. Tell them not to use photographs without permission.

Back at school

Look at some of the completed sheets with the children and talk about how they have changed as they have grown up. Ask the children to look at each other's sheets: would they have recognised their friends as a baby, or have they changed too much?

p33 My family — SCIENCE PRACTICE

Learning objective

- To know that there are different stages in the human life cycle.

Lesson context

Invite adults of different ages into the classroom, and encourage the children to identify some of the different stages in the human life cycle. Discuss some of the physical differences, capabilities and needs of people at various stages in their lives. Ask: *Who needs looking after? What can and can't they do?*

Setting the homework

Ask the children to think about the various members of their family. *Who is the youngest and who is the oldest?* Tell the children that they should draw pictures of their family and try to find out how old each one is to complete the sheet.

Back at school

Ask the children to raise their hands if they have a baby at home who is less than six months old. *Are there any children less than three months old or any new-born babies?* Find the age of the youngest of all. Find the age of the oldest family member in the same way.

p34 Shopping for food and drink — SCIENCE TO SHARE

Learning objectives
- To know that food and water are needed for animals, including humans, to stay alive.
- To carry out a simple survey.

Lesson context
Talk with the children about how food and water are necessary to sustain life. Look at pictures of well-nourished and malnourished children and talk about what happens if people don't have enough food and water. Ask the children if they have ever been really hungry; do they know that other animals also need food and water to remain healthy and alive?

Setting the homework
Set a date about a week later for returning this homework so that all the children have a chance to look at the family shopping depending when the weekly shop is done. Remind the children that it is food and water that are essential to life, but that we sometimes get some of our water by drinking other things such as soft drinks, tea, coffee and so on.

Back at school
Gather the children together and ask some to talk about their pictures to the rest of the class. Have all the children put in *food* and *water* to complete their sentence?

UNIT 2 ANIMALS & PLANTS — GROWING AND CARING

p35 Dead or alive? — SCIENCE PRACTICE

Learning objective
- To know how to distinguish a living thing from a non-living thing.

Lesson context
Discuss with the children the features that distinguish things that are living, no longer living and things that have never been alive, such as a plant, a wooden spoon and a fridge magnet. Encourage the children to sort objects into these different groups, describing processes such as moving, drinking, feeding and breathing, that distinguish living things.

Setting the homework
Ask the children to remind you of some things that are living, no longer living and have never been alive that they talked about in the lesson. Tell them that they should look at home for some things that fit into each category and draw pictures of some of them.

Back at school
Look at some of the things the children found. Make lists under each heading on a board or flip chart, and ask the children to check that things are listed in the correct group.

p36 What is it? — SCIENCE PRACTICE

Learning objective
- To recognise and name some common animals.

Lesson context
Show the children a selection of pictures of animals, including insects, birds and fish, and see if they can name them. Take them out into the local environment to see what different kinds of animals they can see. Encourage them to make a list of the names of all the animals they have observed.

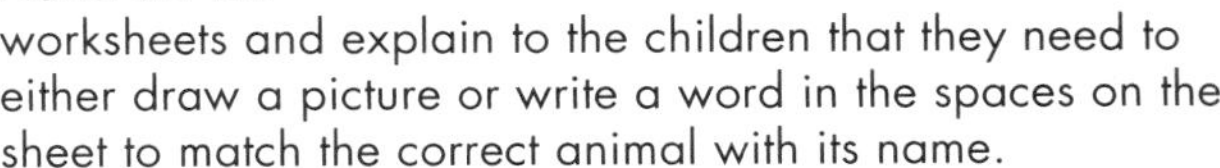

Setting the homework
Hand out the worksheets and explain to the children that they need to either draw a picture or write a word in the spaces on the sheet to match the correct animal with its name.

Back at school
Look at the children's completed sheets. Invite them to tell you about any unusual animals that they have seen recently on the television or while they have been out and about.

p37 Beetle — NUMERACY LINK

Learning objective
- To recognise and name the main external parts of the bodies of animals.

Lesson context
Look at pictures or models of animals and name the main external parts, such as ears, eyes, legs, beaks and tails. Talk about the parts that humans have in common with other animals, and parts that are particular to certain creatures, such as wings, fins and so on.

Setting the homework
Playing 'Beetle' gives children the chance to reinforce numeracy and vocabulary. Explain the rules of the game to the children, and point out that they will need a dice to be able to play. You may like to give the children several days for this activity in order to give them time to play the game at least once.

Back at school
Ask: *Did you enjoy playing the game? Who won? Did anyone invent a new game with a different animal? Can you explain it to the class?*

p38 How do they move? — OBSERVATION

Learning objective
- To know that animals can move in different ways from humans.

Lesson context
Watch, either live or on video, a range of different animals moving. Observe how they swim, run, fly and so on. Compare how animals move with how humans move – can the children move like the animals they are watching?

Setting the homework
Read through the example on the worksheet with the children. Remind them that human beings are animals too, and ask them to think about how they move in comparison to the animals they see. You may wish to set this activity over several days, including a weekend if possible.

Back at school
Ask the children to give you some examples of the animals they have seen. *What did you notice about their movements? Has anyone seen any unusual animals? How did they move in comparison to a human?*

p39 I-spy plants OBSERVATION

Learning objective

- To recognise and name some common plants.

Lesson context

Take the children out on a walk in the local environment and see how many different types of plant (remembering to include grass and trees) they can recognise and name. Encourage them to look particularly at the shape of the leaves and flowers on plants they find.

Setting the homework

Give each child a copy of the worksheet and make sure they understand what they have to do. Ask them to go out and see what plants they can find in their locality. Remind them to look carefully at the shape of the leaves and of any flowers on the plants to help identify them (whether there are flowers or not will depend upon the time of year that you do this activity). You may wish to give the children a few days in which to complete the homework.

Back at school

See who managed to find every plant on the sheet. *Did the shape of the leaves help you to identify the plants or was it just the flowers? Did anybody add more plants of their own?* Ask the children to name any of the trees they have identified.

p40 Growing seeds is fun SCIENCE TO SHARE

Learning objective

- To know that most plants grow from seeds.

Lesson context

Look at a selection of seeds and sort them into different types. See if the children can predict what each type of seed will grow in to, using seed packets for information. Encourage groups of children to plant seeds and keep a diary of their germination and growth.

Setting the homework

Talk about some foods the children may eat that have seeds in them, such as oranges, grapefruit, peppers and so on. Suggest that next time they eat something which has seeds in it they try growing the seeds at home and caring for the baby plants. This homework may be best set over several days; you may wish to return to this activity after a few weeks to see if the children have had any success with growing their plants.

Back at school

Ask the children what sort of seeds they planted. Make a list on a board or flip chart. *What do you need to do to care for your seeds?* Some children could read out what they have written on their sheets.

p41 Sort the tins FINDING OUT

Learning objectives

- To know that plants provide a wide range of foods.
- To be able to match some foods to their plant of origin.

Lesson context

Encourage the children to think about what they ate for breakfast or lunch. See if they can identify any foods that were obtained from plants and match some of these foods to their plant of origin. Talk about how plants can be eaten raw, cooked or both. Try to think of some other foods made from the same plants.

Setting the homework

Remind the children that much of our food comes from plants, but that it often looks different when it has, for example, been made into bread, processed, or put into tins. Ask the children to look at any tins of food they have in the kitchen cupboard at home and to make a list of the ones containing foods made from plants.

Back at school

See what different kinds of food the children managed to find. Can they match the foods to the plant they came from?

p42 Salad for tea LITERACY LINK

Learning objective

- To know that some foods are prepared directly from plants.

Lesson context

Show the children a selection of fruits and see if they can name each one. Sort the fruits according to various criteria, such as colour, shape, whether we peel them or not before eating and so on. Cut the fruit up and prepare and enjoy a fruit salad.

Setting the homework

This activity will develop the children's label-writing skills. Talk about different types of salad, such as green salad, rice, pasta and so on. Remind the children that almost everything in a salad comes from plants. *Do any of you have a favourite salad? What sort of things might you put in a salad?* Ask the children to draw and label these ingredients on their worksheet, and suggest that they help to make a salad for tea at home.

Back at school

Discuss some of the children's salad recipes. *What type of salad were they? What was in them? Did all the ingredients come from plants?* Find out if any of the children made their salad for tea. *What did you need to do to prepare the salad?* Did they wash or mix the salad, for example?

p43 Weather record — NUMERACY LINK

Learning objectives
- To know that there are simple features of the weather that can be observed.
- To collect data.

Lesson context
Using a class weather chart record simple, first-hand observations of the weather each day and talk about what the weather is like. Talk about the weather forecast on TV and why it is important for some people to know what sort of weather to expect, for example farmers need to know whether they can go out and care for their land and pilots need to know whether it's safe to fly.

Setting the homework
Explain that, using the worksheet, the children should record their weather observations twice a day for a week like they might on the class weather chart. Make sure they understand that they should start their record on whatever day the sheet goes home: if you send the sheet home on Thursday, they should begin recording on Thursday evening and make their last observation the following Thursday morning before bringing the sheet back to school.

Back at school
Ask the children to count how many days the weather was different in the afternoon from the morning. Is this fewer or more than the days on which it was the same? If they have time, some children might be able to use the information collected at home to make a block graph.

p44 Blowing in the wind — FINDING OUT

Learning objective
- To make and use a simple wind meter to measure the strength and direction of the wind.

Lesson context
Use plastic strips of different thicknesses so children can make simple wind meters (thicker, heavier strips of plastic will require more wind to make them move, so children can gauge the wind's strength). Children should use their wind meters to measure the strength and direction of the wind out in the playground.

Setting the homework
The day before setting this homework, ask the children to bring in a carrier bag in which to take their wind meters home (collect a few spares yourself for those who forget). Remind the children how their wind meters work, and ask them to measure the strength of the wind at home at the same time each day for a week. On some days there may be no wind, so no streamers will be coloured in on the sheet.

Back at school
Look at the children's completed recording sheets. Ask: *Can you tell from your records which day was the windiest? Were there any days when there was no wind at all? Was the wind blowing from the same direction every day?*

p45 Signs of the seasons – autumn — SCIENCE TO SHARE

Learning objective
- To know how the environment changes as the year passes through the seasons (autumn).

Lesson context
On an autumn day, look at some pictures of autumn scenes with the children and talk about things found in this season (such as falling leaves, berries and lengthening shadows). A 'seasons hoop' (described in *100 Science Lessons: Year 1/Primary 2*, page 70) will help the children appreciate the cyclical nature of the seasons; add the autumn photographs in the appropriate section of the seasons hoop. Together, go out and look for fruits, berries and leaves, and try measuring the length of children's shadows. Talk about what changes during autumn, such as darker evenings.

Setting the homework
Give the children a copy of the worksheet and explain what they should do. Remind them that they should never eat anything they find unless told that it is safe to do so by a responsible adult.

Back at school
See if the children found anything unusual on their walks – were there any fruits they couldn't name? Suggest that they might look these up in books later if they have time. The children's drawings could be added to an autumn display.

p46 Signs of the seasons – winter — OBSERVATION

Learning objective
- To know how the environment changes as the year passes through the seasons (winter).

Lesson context
This lesson follows on from the previous lesson, but needs to be carried out on a winter's day. Revisit the locations of the autumn walk with the children and note any changes in the environment. Compare a winter shadow with an autumn one – have the children noticed whether it is dark when they get up and go to bed? Back in the classroom, compare pictures of autumn and winter scenes, and add new photographs to the seasons hoop.

Setting the homework
Ask the children to look for things at home that tell them it is winter. *What do you do differently? Do you wear different clothes in winter? Do you eat different food? Do you have a fire or put the heating on? Do you play inside or out?*

Back at school
Look at the completed sheets. Choose some children to tell the class about what they have drawn; other children could read their sentences.

p47 Signs of the seasons – spring — OBSERVATION

Learning objective

- To know how the environment changes as the year passes through the seasons (spring).

Lesson context

Following on from the previous two activities, carry this lesson out on a spring day. Take the children out again and notice any changes since their last walk, especially the length of shadows. Look at pictures of springtime and notice any differences between the spring and winter pictures, and add the pictures to the seasons hoop.

Setting the homework

Look at the picture on the worksheet with the children and ask them if they can tell you what season it represents. Explain the activity. Remind them that the signs of spring are all around them, in parks, gardens and the countryside; encourage them to keep their eyes open as they go home.

Back at school

Ask some of the children to name the things they ringed on their picture and explain anything else that they have added. *Did you see anything on the way home that told you it was spring?*

p48 Signs of the seasons – summer — SCIENCE PRACTICE

Learning objective

- To know how the environment changes as the year passes through the seasons (summer).

Lesson context

Complete this series of four lessons on a summer's day. Retrace the walk taken in previous seasons and look once more at what has changed, noticing the difference in shadow length. Compare pictures of spring with pictures of summer and discuss any differences. Add new pictures to complete the seasons hoop.

Setting the homework

Make sure the children can recognise all the pictures provided on the sheet and together read the instructions at the beginning.

Back at school

Ask the children if they managed to identify the 'odd ones out'. Ask: *In which season would you see the odd items out?* One or two children could read out their sentences.

p49 I-spy minibeasts — NUMERACY LINK

Learning objective

- To know the names of some common animals (minibeasts) in the local environment.

Lesson context

Carry out a minibeast safari in a suitable wildlife area (such as the school's wild area or a local park) and encourage the children to look at and think about the habitat of creatures found. Make sure you handle minibeasts with care and respect, using collecting and observation equipment such as pooters and magnifiers, and returning minibeasts to their habitats afterwards. Back in the classroom, identify finds using secondary sources.

Setting the homework

Explain that the children are going to play 'I-spy' to try and find examples of as many creatures listed on the sheet as they can. If they see, for example, several spiders, they may have more than one tick in the 'spiders' box. Remind them to handle any creatures with care and respect. You may wish to give the children time over a weekend to complete this homework.

Back at school

See how the children's minibeast safaris went. Ask: *Did anybody manage to find an example of everything on the sheet? Was any creature more common than another? Was there a creature that no one found? Did anyone find a creature that was not on the list?*

p50 Feed the birds — SCIENCE TO SHARE

Learning objective

- To know the names of some common animals (birds) in the local environment.

Lesson context

Put out some food for birds on a bird table or feeder, and let the children watch the visitors to the table from afar. See if they can learn to recognise and name the different species that visit and keep a simple tally record over time.

Setting the homework

You may like to set this homework over a period of time, such as a month or more. It requires a fair amount of preparation, so you may like to warn helpers of what is required. Explain the activity to the children (stress that they will need an adult to help with the cutting). Ask them to keep a record of any birds that come to the feeder and of any others that they see.

Back at school

If you have set this task over, say, a month, check at intervals whether or not the children have seen any birds. Can they identify any of them? At the end of the time, make a class list of all kinds of bird seen by the children and see which ones were seen most and least often.

p51 My bedroom — LITERACY LINK

Learning objective

- To know that a habitat is a relatively small part of the environment and is the home of a particular plant or animal.

Lesson context

As a class, 'adopt' a tree in the local environment, and encourage the children to look at the tree over a period of time. Talk about how the tree provides a habitat for lots of different animals, particularly minibeasts, and see if the children can find any creatures living in the habitat. Explain that animals live where they do because it provides their food source and the conditions that they need to live.

Setting the homework

Explain to the children that their home is their habitat, and that their bedroom is their own particular part of that habitat. Like some other animals they may share their habitat with others (brothers or sisters). Ask them to complete the sheet.

Back at school

Share some of the children's pictures with the whole class, perhaps making a class book.

UNIT 4 MATERIALS | PROPERTIES OF MATERIALS

p52 What's it like? LITERACY LINK

Learning objective
- To know that different materials have different properties.

Lesson context
Let the children handle and examine a variety of different materials (wood, rock and different kinds of plastic, for example) and see if they can think of words to describe them. Together, sort the materials into groups according to given and to their own criteria, such as flexible, transparent and so on. Practise possible new vocabulary such as flexible, transparent and opaque.

Setting the homework
Make sure the children can read and understand what each property listed on the sheet is. Tell them that some materials may fit into more than one category, but that they need to decide which box to put them in.

Back at school
Write the categories on the board or flip chart. Ask the children to name some of the materials they found in each group. Discuss any particularly good examples and see if anybody put a material, for example glass, in different categories – does the material in question have more than one property?

p53 What's it made from? SCIENCE PRACTICE

Learning objective
- To be able to identify some common materials.

Lesson context
Show the children some objects, for example a newspaper, plastic beaker or pencil, and ask them to name and label the material each is made from (not the name of the object).

Setting the homework
Make sure that the children understand that it is examples of the material they are looking for, and that the object itself is not important.

Back at school
Look at the completed worksheets. Check that the children have found at least one object in each category. Were any of the groups hard to find something for?

p54 Is it magnetic? FINDING OUT

Learning objective
- To know that some materials are magnetic, but most are not.

Lesson context
Talk about certain materials being magnetic and others not. Show the children a range of materials (wood, plastic, paper clips and so on) and ask them to predict, then test whether or not they are magnetic. Help the children to begin to understand that not all materials are magnetic, but those that are attracted to a magnet are metal.

Setting the homework
You will need to give each child a small piece of magnetic tape for this activity. Explain that they should use this to make a list of things at home that are magnetic. You could suggest some places to look if the children are struggling – fridge doors are often kept closed with magnets.
Encourage them to use their imaginations to answer the last question, thinking of something they could do if they had a really big, strong magnet.

Back at school
Ask the children to name some of the things that were attracted to their magnets. Make a list on a board or flip chart and point out that all the magnetic things are made from metal. Share some of the children's ideas about uses for their giant magnets.

p55 More of the same NUMERACY LINK

Learning objectives
- To know that a range of materials are used in our environment.
- To know that materials can be used in a variety of ways.

Lesson context
Take the children on a 'materials walkabout' around the school, looking for objects made from different materials (plastic, wood, glass and so on). Discuss why the properties of some materials make them suitable for specific purposes. Talk about the fact that the same material can be used to make different objects.

Setting the homework
Make sure the children understand the words on the sheet and know what they have to do.

Back at school

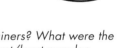

Prepare a sheet or board with names of objects down one axis and possible materials (glass, wood, plastic, and so on) along the other. Ask the children to put up their hands if they found, for example, a glass bowl and enter the number in the appropriate section. Ask: *How many different materials did you find that had been used to make boxes or containers? What were the boxes used for? Which was the most/least popular material?* Add any others materials if necessary.

p56 How many things? SCIENCE PRACTICE

Learning objective
- To know that different objects can be made from the same material.

Lesson context
Sort a collection of objects made from different materials into sets by object: all the cups, all the spoons and so on. Re-sort the objects according to the material from which they are made: all the metal objects, all the pottery objects and so on. Discuss why different materials have been used.

Setting the homework
Explain that the children should choose one material from the list on their sheet and look around their home, both inside and out, to find as many things made from that material as they can.

Back at school
For each material on the sheet, ask children who chose that material to tell the class some of the things they found at home made from that material.

p57 How many materials? — LITERACY LINK

Learning objective

- To know that an object can be made of several materials.

Lesson context

Look at a selection of objects made from several materials. Identify the materials used and discuss how their use is related to the properties of the material.

Setting the homework

This activity allows children to practise their labelling and writing skills. Recap how to label a drawing by labelling the materials used on a simple picture of your own drawn on a board or flip chart.

Back at school

Talk about some of the objects the children have chosen and the materials used to make them. Use the pictures to make a display.

p58 Is it waterproof? — SCIENCE TO SHARE

Learning objectives

- To carry out a simple investigation with help.
- To know that some materials are waterproof and others are not.

Lesson context

Using a range of different waterproof and non-waterproof materials, help the children plan and carry out a simple investigation to find out what would be the best material for making an umbrella.

Setting the homework

Explain the worksheet to the children. Make sure they understand that they must carry out this activity with their helper to avoid Mum's best hat being taken into the bath!

Back at school

Talk with the children about their experiments. Ask them about some of the things they tested: *Were they all waterproof? How could you tell? Why did they need to be waterproof? Did you have fun?*

p59 Egg sandwiches — LITERACY LINK

Learning objective

- To know that some materials can be changed by forces.

Lesson context

Let the children see how forces can change the shape of a material by giving them lumps of play dough to stretch, roll, squash and shape. Ask them to decide whether they are using a push or pull to change the shape of dough.

Setting the homework

You might like to warn helpers in advance that they will need specific ingredients for this activity. Read through the recipe on the worksheet with the children. Stress the fact that they must have an adult to help with this activity because boiling water and knives can be dangerous.

Back at school

Look at some of the children's pictures of them enjoying their sandwiches. Ask them to tell you how the shape of the egg was changed. *What type of force were you using (pull or push)?*

UNIT 5 ELECTRICITY — USING & MISUSING ELECTRICITY

p60 Electrical things — SCIENCE PRACTICE

Learning objective

- To know that many appliances need electricity to make them work.

Lesson context

Look around the classroom for equipment that needs electricity to make it work. Make a list of things that do and do not need electricity. Demonstrate how electrical appliances need to be plugged in and switched on before they will work, reinforcing the dangers of electricity.

Setting the homework

Explain the worksheet to the children; encourage them to look for less obvious items in the house that use mains electricity (not batteries).

Back at school

See what different electrical equipment the class managed to find. Was there anything unusual? Were they surprised about how many things use electricity?

p61 Batteries — SCIENCE PRACTICE

Learning objective

- To know that electricity is obtained from the mains or from batteries (cells).

Lesson context

Look at a battery (cell), and some devices that require batteries in order to operate, with the children. Sort the equipment into sets: things that use batteries and those that use mains electricity. Discuss equipment that could use either, such as radios or laptop computers.

Setting the homework

Show the children how to complete the sheet.

Back at school

Make a list on a board or flip chart of all the different battery-powered devices the children have found.

p62 Electricity Snakes and Ladders — SCIENCE TO SHARE

Learning objective

- To know that electricity can be dangerous and must be treated with extreme care.

Lesson context

Talk with the children about the dangers of electricity. Together, devise a set of rules for using electricity safely and make posters illustrating the rules. If you have time, play the game in groups before the children take it home.

Setting the homework

Give each child a worksheet. Explain the rules, and that they will need dice and counters to play the game. (Buttons or pebbles could be used instead of counters, and a spinner instead of dice.) Tell the children that they need not bring the sheets back to school, and they can play the game again. You could set this activity over a weekend or longer to allow the children time to play the game.

Back at school

Ask: *Who did you play the game with? Who won? Was it fun? Can you remember some of the dangers to avoid?*

UNIT 6 FORCES & MOTION | INTRODUCING FORCES

p63 Me moving — SCIENCE PRACTICE

Learning objective

- To know that there are different kinds of movement.

Lesson context

Take the children into the playground and ask them to move from one side to another in as many ways as they can (running, hopping, on hands and feet, and so on). Encourage them to think about which parts of their bodies they are using. Ask the children to draw themselves moving across the playground, then make a class display of the pictures and create a tally chart of different movements.

Setting the homework

Ask the children to draw themselves moving in a different way from the picture they drew in class.

Back at school

Share the children's pictures and ask them to talk about what they are doing in their drawings. Ask: *Can you describe the force you were using?* Collect the pictures and make a class 'movement' display.

p64 Using forces to move things — SCIENCE PRACTICE

Learning objectives

- To know that forces, such as pushes and pulls, can move objects and change their direction.
- To begin to understand cause and effect.

Lesson context

Using a variety of PE equipment, let the children experience how forces can make things move and change direction, for example by throwing and catching balls or beanbags, or pulling gently against one another on a skipping rope. Encourage them to use vocabulary such as *push, pull* and *force* when describing what they are doing.

Setting the homework

Recap with the children a few everyday activities that use forces (opening a door, for example). Explain that you want them to think of as many activities as they can for each force on the sheet, and that they can describe them in either words or pictures.

Back at school

Ask some of the children to demonstrate some of the actions they added to their sheet. *What force were you using?* (Push, pull or twist?)

p65 Using forces to change a shape — SCIENCE PRACTICE

Learning objective

- To know that forces such as pushes, pulls and twists can change the shape of objects.

Lesson context

Help the children to make cheese straws, working in groups. There is a recipe on page 143 of *100 Science Lessons: Year 1/Primary 2*, or you may have a recipe in one of your own cookery books that the children can use. As they are doing this, draw their attention to the forces they are using to change the shape of the dough.

Setting the homework

Help the children to identify each picture on the sheet and make sure that they know what pushing, pulling, squeezing and twisting forces are.

Back at school

Go through the answers. Ask the children to mark their own sheets, ticking the things they have correctly drawn in the box as you call them out. Can they tell you why they left the other things out?

p66 Blow football — SCIENCE TO SHARE

Learning objectives

- To consider the wind as a force.
- To know that wind is moving air.
- To know that the wind can make things move.

Lesson context

Take the children outside on a breezy day and blow bubbles to see them floating about. What does this show them about the wind? Talk about other ways in which we can tell that the wind is blowing.

Setting the homework

Ask the children to blow gently on their hands to feel the moving air. Give each child two straws so you are sure that everybody can play the game at home. (A ping-pong ball is useful for the activity, but a screwed-up ball of paper works just as well.) Tell them that they could write the score down on their sheet but they need not bring it back to school.

Back at school

Talk about how the children played the game. *Did you have fun? Who won? Was it easy to direct the moving air to push the ball into the goal?*

p67 Pushing down and pushing up — FINDING OUT

Learning objectives

- To experience the upward push (force) of water.
- To know that water pushes upwards on objects.

Lesson context

Let the children investigate floating by pushing various objects that float (for example, cork, balsa wood and balloons) into a tank of water and feeling the water pushing up. Talk about what they can feel. *Which object is the most difficult to push under the water?*

Setting the homework

Read through the sheet with the children and make sure they understand what they have to do.

Back at school

Talk about the investigation: *Which objects sank? Which floated? Which object was the most difficult to push under the water? Can anyone tell me how the water helps some things to float?*

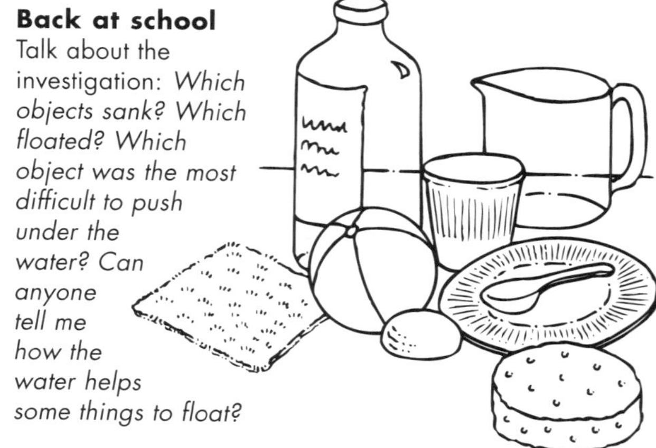

p68 In the dark — FINDING OUT

Learning objective

- To know that light is needed for us to see things.

Lesson context

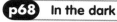

Talk about experiences that the children may have had of dark places. Look at an object (say, a teddy bear) in a dark box (see diagram below) and ask whether the children can see it. Gradually let more light into the box and encourage them to describe what they can see at each stage.

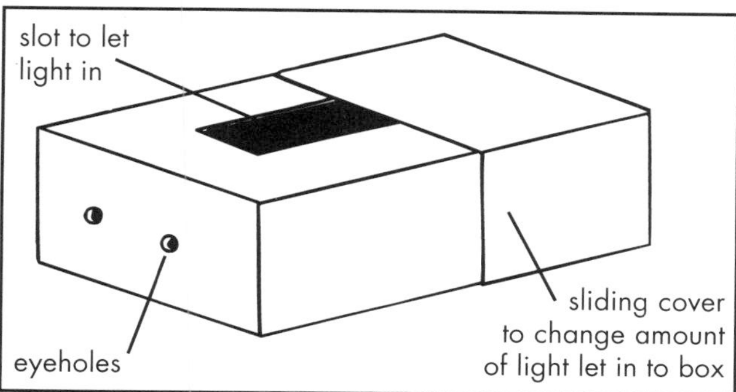

Setting the homework

Explain to the children that they will need to close the door and the curtains to make their room as dark as possible for this activity.

Back at school

Ask: *What could you see when your bedroom was light? Could you see more or less when the room was dark?* See whether anybody played 'Blindfold tag'. *Could you see anything with the blindfold on? Why not?* (A blindfold prevents light entering the eye.)

 Light — NUMERACY LINK

Learning objective

- To know that there are many sources of light.

Lesson context

Look at a variety of different light sources (including oil lamps, torches and pictures of the Sun), then walk with the children around school, inside and outside, noting where lights are placed. Discuss why we need light and what sources of light people used before electricity. How is light useful to us?

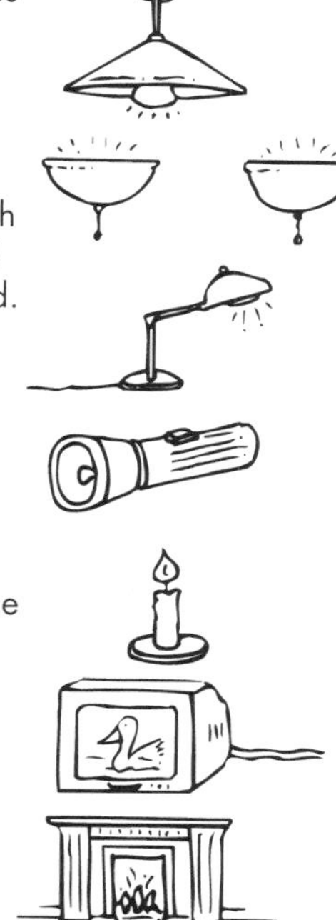

Setting the homework

Explain the worksheet to the children, saying that not all possible sources of light are on the chart, but there is space for them to add any others they find.

Back at school

Find out which light source was most common, and which least. (You might like to make a block graph or pictogram.) Talk about any other light sources the children found: *What are they used for? What was the most unusual light source anybody found?*

p70 Very bright — LITERACY LINK

Learning objective

- To know that light sources vary in brightness.

Lesson context

Help the children carry out an investigation to test a number of torches, finding out which is the brightest by reading by torchlight in a darkened corner. Discuss ways of designing a fair test.

Setting the homework

Ask the children to think about the lights they have at home and what they are used for. Why might they need a bright light? When would a dim light be sufficient? Ask the children to look for the brightest and dimmest lights they can find at home and to write a sentence about what they are used for.

Back at school

Ask some children to read out their sentences. *Why would you need a bright light? When would you use only a dim light?*

p71 In an emergency — SCIENCE PRACTICE

Learning objective

- To know how to call the emergency services.

Lesson context

Talk about keeping safe at a bonfire or fireworks party. Use role-play to help the children learn how to call the emergency services when at home.

Setting the homework

Remind the children of the role-play when they called the emergency services. Explain the worksheet to the children. Reiterate that they should call the emergency services *only* in a real emergency.

Back at school

Go through the answers and ask the children to put up their hands if they chose the correct service. Collect in the worksheets and check that each child has written their address correctly. Remember not to display any work that shows the children's addresses or phone numbers.

p72 Sounds at home — SCIENCE PRACTICE

Learning objective

- To know that there are many different sources of sound in the locality.

Lesson context

Take the children on a 'sound walk' in the local area and ask them to note down any sounds they can hear. Talk about the sources of some of the sounds.

Setting the homework

Ask the children to sit completely silently and listen for a short time. *What can you hear?* Ask them to do the same at home and complete the worksheet.

Back at school

Go through some of the sounds the children heard. Were there any unusual ones? Was there a sound that everyone heard, such as people talking, the television, traffic?

p73 Making music — SCIENCE TO SHARE

Learning objective

- To identify some objects that make sounds.

Lesson context

Collect pictures of things that make sounds and ask the children to label the pictures with the noise they make. Think about the purpose of the sound (is it a warning, for information, to have fun?)

Setting the homework

Make sure the children understand what they have to do, and that they should ask an adult to help them choose the items for this activity so as not to use any breakable items as instruments. Ask for some ideas of things they might use to make a sound.

Back at school

Talk with the class about some of the things they used as instruments and the sounds they made. Were they able to make a tune? Listen to any tapes that may have been brought in.

p74 Nasty noises — SCIENCE PRACTICE

Learning objectives

- To know that a 'noise' is often an unpleasant sound.
- To know that loud noises can be harmful.

Lesson context

Play the children a short tape of gentle music. Did they find it pleasant or unpleasant? Talk about different sounds and what makes them pleasant or unpleasant. Look at a pair of ear defenders. What would they be used for? Talk about the possibility of loud noises damaging hearing. Hit your largest cymbal as hard as you can. Ask the children to put up their hands if they liked the sound. *Did anybody not like it? Why not?*

Setting the homework

Explain the sheet to the children. Emphasise that they may not all find the same sounds pleasant or unpleasant – your own dog barking may be nice to you, but may annoy your neighbour.

Back at school

Ask the children what sounds they liked or disliked. *Were there any sounds some of you liked but others didn't? Can you explain why you like a particular sound and not another?*

p75 Helpful sounds — LITERACY LINK

Learning objective

- To know that our hearing helps to keep us safe.

Lesson context

Discuss warning sounds such as pedestrian crossings, fire alarms and sirens, and how they help to keep us safe. Take the children outside and listen to traffic sounds to show that we need our ears as well as our eyes to keep us safe when, for example, crossing roads. Ask the children to close their eyes and see what they can hear: *What does it tell you about nearby traffic?* Reinforce the idea of road safety.

Setting the homework

This activity will help children's writing skills. Explain the sheet to the children, and tell them that it will take a week to complete. They can include any warning sounds they hear, both indoors and out.

Back at school

Look at the children's results: *Who heard some kind of warning sound each day? Were there any days on which you heard no warnings? Why did some of you hear more than others? Do you perhaps live near a main road? Does Mum or Dad saying, 'I'm warning you!' count?*

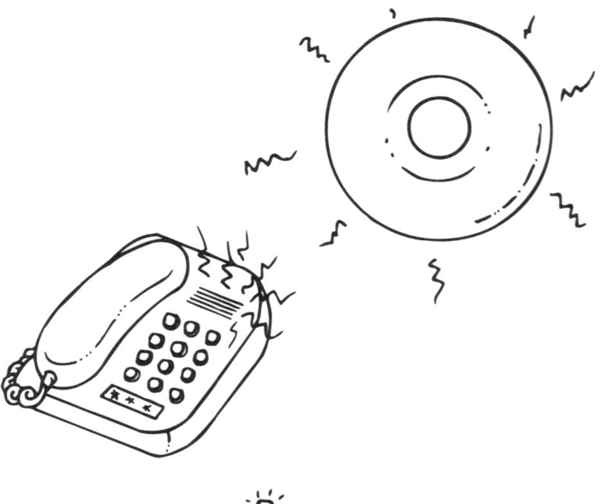

UNIT 8 EARTH & BEYOND — STARGAZING

p76 Moon watch — LITERACY LINK

Learning objectives

- To know that the Moon is a sphere.
- To know that the Moon appears to change its shape.

Lesson context

Ask the children what shape they think the Moon is. Show them how the Moon only *appears* to change shape by moving a large ball around the light from an OHP – they can only see the lit portion, but the shape of the Moon stays the same. Ask the children to draw the different phases of the Moon. If it's the right time of year/month, take them outside to observe the Moon in the sky.

Setting the homework

This homework will take a month to complete. Make sure the children understand that it doesn't matter if they can't see the Moon on a particular day because of cloud but to try again the next day. Make sure they look for the Moon at roughly the same time each day.

Back at school

At the end of the survey, find out how many times the children managed to see the Moon (it may have been a very cloudy month!). *Did anybody notice an apparent change in its shape? Can anyone remember why the Moon seems to change shape?* Check which shape the children have coloured in at the bottom of the sheet. Reinforce the fact that the Moon is a sphere and does not actually change its shape.

p77 Sun, Moon and stars — SCIENCE PRACTICE

Learning objective

- To distinguish the Sun and the Moon from the stars.

Lesson context

Watch a tealight burn in a darkened room and discuss how this is like our Sun burning. Talk about how the other stars in the sky are also like this, but they are so far away that they appear to be tiny in the sky. Talk about when we can see the stars, Moon and Sun.

Setting the homework

Remind the children that our Sun is a star like the others we can see in the sky, but seems big because it is much nearer. Explain how to complete the sheet.

Back at school

Check that the children have stuck the star shape over the Sun. Ask them to make sure they have the following sentences completed:

Our Sun is a star.
We see most stars as tiny dots of light because they are so far away *(or similar words)*.
The Sun is our nearest star.

p78 Night work — ASK AN ADULT

Learning objective

- To know that the pattern of day and night affects animals.

Lesson context

Talk about animals that are active at night, and see if the children can suggest why this may be. Discuss how human beings are normally awake during the day and asleep at night, but that some people have to work at night. How do the children think it may affect these people and how do they think they cope with it?

Setting the homework

Ask the children if they know anyone who works at night. What do they do? Tell the children that you want them to ask an adult and find out about other night-time jobs that people do.

Back at school

Ask the children to tell you some of the night-time jobs they have found out about. How many different ones did they think of altogether? Make a list on a board or flip chart.

p79 Food groups — SCIENCE PRACTICE

Learning objectives

- To know that food can be put into different groups.
- To understand that a knowledge of food groups can help us to build healthy diets.

Lesson context

Find out some of the children's favourite foods, and sort them into four different groups (meat, fish, eggs and dairy products; fruit and vegetables; cereals; high-energy foods). Talk about a balanced diet comprising elements from each of these food groups, and about how no food is 'bad' unless we eat too much of it.

Setting the homework

Remind the children of the names of the four different food groups and ask them to suggest a food that could go in each of the groups. Explain the sheet to the children.

Back at school

Ask the children to tell you some of the foods they have put into each group. Make class lists on a board or flip chart and talk about any of the foods that could be put into more than one group.

p80 Exercise diary — LITERACY LINK

Learning objective

- To know that regular exercise is needed to maintain good health.

Lesson context

Discuss how regular exercise is needed to keep healthy, and about the kinds of exercise the children enjoy. During a PE lesson, stop the children occasionally and ask them to think about what they are doing and the muscles they are using and developing. Can they name the parts of the body that they are exercising?

Setting the homework

You may want to send this worksheet home a week before carrying out the lesson. Ask the children to fill in the diary every day (you may need to remind them during the week). Make sure they understand what *regular exercise* means.

Back at school

Ask some of the children to tell you about the exercise they did at home. Which was their favourite? Which exercise was most common? Was there an overall favourite?

p81 Sleep diary — NUMERACY LINK

Learning objective

- To know that enough and regular sleep is needed for good health.

Lesson context

Talk about why we need sufficient and regular sleep in order to let our bodies and brains rest and develop. Discuss how lack of sleep can have adverse effects on our bodies and brains.

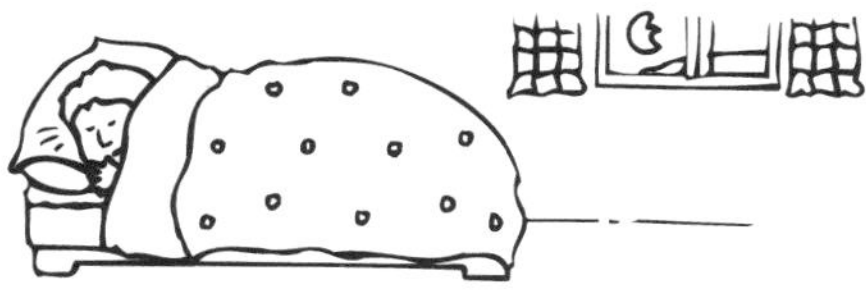

Setting the homework
Explain the diary sheet to the children. Tell them that if they have difficulty in telling the time they should ask their helper.

Back at school
Once the diaries have been completed, ask the children to share their results. How many go to bed at the same time every night? Do they get up at the same time every day to get ready for school? Is it different on Saturdays and Sundays? Have any children worked out how much time they slept over the whole week? Who slept for the longest/ shortest time during the week?

p82 Cleaning teeth — SCIENCE TO SHARE

Learning objective
- To know that the mouth needs care and attention to keep it healthy.

Lesson context
Talk about why our teeth are important and what we do with them. Discuss how to look after teeth and gums to keep them healthy by eating a healthy, balanced diet (including milk) and by brushing teeth regularly. Talk about the importance of regular visits to the dentist.

Setting the homework
This homework will need a week to complete. Ask the children if they know the name of the toothpaste they use. Tell them that they are going to look carefully at their toothpaste and toothbrush so that they can do a really detailed drawing. Explain the rest of the sheet to the children, saying that they should tick the boxes to show when they clean their teeth.

Back at school
Share some of the pictures that the children have drawn. (They could be cut out and used to make a class display.) Reinforce how important the regular cleaning of teeth is.

p83 Bath time — SCIENCE TO SHARE

Learning objective
- To know that the skin needs to be kept clean for good health.

Lesson context
Talk with the children about the importance of keeping clean and the dangers of dirty skin: that it can spread germs and lead to infection. Talk about people who need to keep their hands especially clean because of the job they do (such as doctors or people who work with food).

Setting the homework
Ask the children whether they have baths or showers at home. Tell them that next time they have a bath or shower they should think carefully about what they are doing, and then talk to their helper about what they do to keep themselves really clean.

Back at school
Share some of the children's pictures. Ask some children to read out the list of things they use to keep themselves clean. Can anyone tell you why it is important to keep clean?

p84 People who care — FINDING OUT

Learning objective
- To know that young humans need care while they are growing up.

Lesson context
Talk about how parents help their children as they are growing up (feeding them, keeping them clean, talking to them and so on). Ask a parent with different-aged children to come and talk to the class about what they have to do to look after children of different ages.

Setting the homework
This homework will need a few days to complete. Explain the sheet to the children, and try to think of a few more examples that they could fill in. Tell them that it doesn't matter if they don't fill every space.

Back at school
Ask the children to tell you some of the things grown-ups or older brothers and sisters have done for them. Are they surprised by how much people do for them? Have they done anything in the last few days to care for anyone else?

p85 How we change — ASK AN ADULT

Learning objective
- To know that our appearance changes over time.

Lesson context
Read 'The Seven Ages of Man' from Shakespeare's *As You Like It*. See if the children can identify the stages of life that human beings go through from birth to death, noting the children's ideas about changes (especially in appearance) at each stage. Make a class list of their ideas.

Setting the homework
Ask the children if they know an old person (it could be Grandma or Granddad). Can they tell you one or two ways in which they look different from themselves? Explain that they should ask an older person questions about how they have changed as they have become older, and use the sheet to make notes and a drawing.

Back at school
Share some of the children's notes and pictures. What are the most common changes as people age?

p86 Plant or animal? SCIENCE PRACTICE

Learning objective

- To know the difference between an animal and a plant.

Lesson context

Prepare a set of questions that the children can use to decide whether an object is an animal or a plant (for example, can it see? can it move? does it live forever? can it feel?). Look at a plant and a small animal and use the questions to distinguish between the two.

Setting the homework

Give out the worksheets and make sure the children understand what they have to do.

Back at school

Mark the sheets with the children and ask them to tell you some of the ways in which plants and animals are different.

p87 Animal or plant? SCIENCE PRACTICE

Learning objective

- To sort a group of living things into animals or plants.

Lesson context

Look at a selection of pictures of plants and animals (include plants, mammals, insects, fish and birds in your selection). Ask the children whether they are plant or animal and sort them into groups. Discuss the characteristics of plants and the things that animals have in common.

Setting the homework

Look at the picture together and ask the children to identify one or two animals and plants, as practice.

Back at school

Ask the children how many plants and how many animals they found (8 animals and 10 plants). Can they name any of them?

p88 My plant LITERACY LINK

Learning objective

- To know how to use secondary sources to find out about plants.

Lesson context

Ask the children to use different sources of information to find out about a group of plants (such as conifers, ferns, flowering plants) and present their findings to the class in a variety of ways.

Setting the homework

Tell the children that they should choose one plant each to research at home, and ask them to complete the sheet, using books, magazines or the Internet to find their information. Suggest that they might like to go to the library to find books.

Back at school

Look at some of the children's completed sheets. Where did they find the information? The sheets could be used to make a class reference book.

p89 At the supermarket SCIENCE TO SHARE

Learning objective

- To know that there are many different types of fruits and seeds.

Lesson context

Look at a selection of different fruits and their seeds, comparing the shapes and sizes of the seeds. Discuss how some seeds are spread by animals or the wind. Warn the children about not eating any fruits or berries unless they are told it is safe to do so by a responsible adult.

Setting the homework

This homework may need a few days to complete. Ask the children to look for fruits, seeds, nuts and pulses while out shopping. Tell them to list as many as they can on their sheet and write about the best way to eat or cook their favourite fruit, seed, nut or pulse. Perhaps some could bring in a sample!

Back at school

See if anybody found an unusual fruit, seed, nut or pulse, or one they had never seen before. Ask some children to read out their lists. Share some favourite ways of eating what they chose.

p90 Seedy? SCIENCE TO SHARE

Learning objective

- To know that different fruits contain different numbers of seeds.

Lesson context

Look at a selection of different fruits and berries. Ask pairs of children to count the seeds in each and to produce a simple graph that shows which contains the most seeds.

Setting the homework

This homework will need a week to complete. Ask the children to tell you some of their favourite fruits. Can they tell you whether they contain seeds or not? Explain the sheet, and that they can include things like tomatoes, cucumbers, or anything else that contains seeds.

Back at school

Talk about some of the things the children ate this week that had seeds in them. *Did anybody eat anything unusual? What had the most seeds? Did anybody plant any seeds?* Ask them to tell you when the seeds start to grow.

p91 Animal groups SCIENCE PRACTICE

Learning objective

- To know that animals can be sorted into groups.

Lesson context

Look at a selection of pictures of animals (including examples of mammals, insects, fish, birds and reptiles). Talk about each creature and its characteristics before assigning it to one of the five groups. See if the children can think of other animals to add to each group.

Setting the homework

Briefly recap on the characteristics that define each group, and explain the sheet to the children.

Back at school

Mark the sheet with the children and make sure they have sorted the pictures correctly. Remind them of some of the characteristics that define each group of creatures.

p92 Native animals — LITERACY LINK

Learning objective

- To know how to use secondary sources to find out about a wide range of animals.

Lesson context

Ask the children to choose an unusual animal and prepare a presentation that they have researched using secondary sources. They can work individually or in pairs.

Setting the homework

This activity may take a few days to complete. Make sure the children understand that they are to choose an animal that is native to this country for the activity. Remind them that they should not copy out sections of text, but look for interesting facts about their animal to complete the sheet.

Back at school

Talk about the animals the children have chosen. Ask one or two to read out their notes. Where did they find their information? You might like to make the sheets into a class reference book.

p93 Butterfly changes — FINDING OUT

Learning objective

- To know that animals reproduce and change as they grow older.

Lesson context

Read the Big Book *Tadpole Diary* by David Drew (Rigby) and talk about all the changes that take place as tadpoles develop into frogs.

Setting the homework

Give out the worksheets and explain that the children should colour and order the pictures to tell the story of a butterfly's life.

Back at school

Check that the children have ordered the pictures correctly (eggs, caterpillar, chrysalis, butterfly), and that they were able to label the different stages. Did anyone look for and find any caterpillars, butterflies, moths or chrysalises?

UNIT 3 THE ENVIRONMENT — LIFE IN HABITATS

p94 I-spy plants and animals — OBSERVATION

Learning objective

- To know the names of some of the plants and animals in the local environment.

Lesson context

Talk about what plants and animals you might expect to see in the local environment, and where they might be found. Take the children out and encourage them to collect, sketch or photograph examples of plants and animals they find. Remind the children of the need to take care of the local environment.

Setting the homework

Tell the children that they are going to play 'I-spy plants and animals'. Read through the sheet (you might like to adapt the list to suit the local area) and explain that they should look out for each thing over the next week, and write down when they saw it.

Back at school

Did anybody see everything on the list? Ask some children to read out the things they have added to the list. Was there anything on the list that nobody saw?

p95 Comparing plants — OBSERVATION

Learning objective

- To know that plants in the local environment are similar to each other in some ways and different in others.

Lesson context

In groups, ask the children to compare a dandelion, a buttercup and a daisy, noting down similarities and differences between each. Look particularly at the leaves, flowers and seeds.

Setting the homework

Give out the sheets and make sure the children understand what they have to do. Tell them that the plants they choose may not have all the things on the sheet, but they should draw what they can see. If one plant has flowers and one does not, this could be a difference between the two.

Back at school

Ask some of the children to describe some of the similarities and differences between the plants they chose.

p96 Seashore — FINDING OUT

Learning objective

- To know some of the plants and animals in a named habitat.

Lesson context

Show the children how to use a range of collecting equipment (pooters, pond nets, white collecting trays and so on), and how to make detailed observations of plants and animals in a habitat. Go to a specific habitat (such as the school pond or the playing field) and ask the children to record what they find, taking care not to damage the environment.

Setting the homework

Look together at the worksheet and make sure the children can identify the various elements in the picture. Think of some creatures or plants you might find in this habitat, then ask the children to complete the sheet at home.

Back at school

Ask the children to tell you the names of some of the things they found that live on the seashore. Make a class display of the pictures.

p97 Who needs what? — SCIENCE TO SHARE

Learning objective

- To know that living things in a habitat depend on each other.

Lesson context

Ask the children to think about who they depend on in their habitat (their home). Consider the habitats looked at in

previous lessons and talk about any interdependence between plants and animals. Make a habitat display that shows how creatures depend on each other in a habitat.

Setting the homework
Explain the sheet to the children and make sure that they can identify the creatures. Remind them of some of the differences between living and non-living things.

Back at school
Ask the children to read out their writing for each animal. *Does anyone disagree or have anything to add to the list?*

p98 Seasonal change — SCIENCE PRACTICE

Learning objective
- To know that plants and animals change in appearance and behaviour with the seasons.

Lesson context
Talk in detail with the children about the changes that happen to a tree over a year, and how they might affect any creatures that depend on the tree as part of their habitat. Ask the children to draw a set of pictures that illustrate a tree through the seasons.

Setting the homework
Remind the children of the pictures they drew (or let them take them home); these may help them to complete the first part of the sheet. Suggest that it might be fun to play a game with their helper before they stick the pictures on the sheet.

Back at school
Ask the children to check that they have stuck their pictures in the right order.

p99 In my street — SCIENCE TO SHARE

Learning objective
- To know ways in which the environment can be cared for.

Lesson context
Go back and visit one of the areas the children looked at earlier in this unit. Carry out a survey, looking for damage to trees, bushes and paths. Look for evidence of graffiti or other damage. Talk about how what they have seen might affect wildlife in the area. Are there any signs that the area *is* being cared for?

Setting the homework
Tell the children that they should look around their neighbourhood and carry out a survey to see how well the environment is cared for, filling in their sheet accordingly.

Back at school
Ask the children if they think their environment is well-cared for or not. Ask: *What evidence shows this? How could you improve the environment?* If there is a specific problem, children could perhaps write to the council with some ideas for improvements (or indeed write to congratulate the council if that is appropriate!).

p100 Look for labels — FINDING OUT

Learning objective
- To know that fabrics are made from different materials.

Lesson context
Look at a collection of fabrics and identify the materials they are made from. Talk about simple properties of the fabrics and how some are natural while others are manufactured. Let the children look closely at some of the fabrics and see if they can work out what they might be useful for (stretchy lycra or warm wool, for example).

Setting the homework
Ask the children if they can find the label in their school jumper or cardigan. What is the fabric made from? Explain that they are going to do this activity at home with some more of their clothes to see what they are made from.

Back at school
Make a list of the materials the children found. Which was most common? Were there any unusual materials?

p101 Useful materials — SCIENCE PRACTICE

Learning objective
- To know about everyday uses of some materials.

Lesson context
Ask the children to carry out a 'materials survey' around the school, in groups, making a list of all the materials they can find. (Watch out for plastics that look like other materials, or painted surfaces that may disguise wood or metal.) Discuss why some of the materials have been chosen for a particular job.

Setting the homework
Read through the worksheet with the children; make sure they know what they need to look for at home.

Back at school
Find out if everyone found something made from each material. How many things did people find in each group? Which was the biggest group? Why have the materials been chosen for the job they do?

p102 Natural materials — LITERACY LINK

Learning objective
- To know that some materials occur naturally.

Lesson context
Look at a collection of objects made from natural materials (wood, stone and cotton, for example), name the materials and talk about where they come from, using pictures of such things as trees, quarries and cotton fields to show the children the source of the material.

Setting the homework
Tell the children they should look around at home for things that are made from natural materials. Recap the names of some of the materials you have been talking about, and suggest that they might want to look outside as well.

Back at school
Share some of the children's drawings and talk about what they found. Ask other children to read out what they have written about where some natural materials came from.

p103 It's not natural — SCIENCE TO SHARE

Learning objective
- To know that some materials are not natural but are manufactured.

Lesson context
Look at a collection of materials (such as metal alloys, glass, paper, concrete and plastic), and talk about where the children think these come from, linking them to pictures of factories, chemical and steel works to suggest that they are manufactured.

Setting the homework
Remind the children that they have already looked around the home for things made from natural materials; explain that this time they should look for manufactured materials, particularly any that have been used to build their home.

Back at school
Look at some of the children's completed sheets. Talk about any manufactured materials they found and how they were used.

p104 Potato nests — SCIENCE TO SHARE

Learning objective
- To know that materials often change when they are heated.

Lesson context
In small groups, help the children to make small cakes (there is a recipe on page 117 of *100 Science Lessons: Year 2/Primary 3*, or use your favourite cake recipe), and compare the cooked ingredients with the raw ones. Note the changes brought about by the cooking (heating) process, and ask the children if they think it's possible to get the original ingredients back from the cakes.

Setting the homework
This activity requires a fair amount of preparation, so you might like to warn helpers in advance of what will be needed and allow extra time for the children to carry out the task. Read through the recipe and remind the children that they should look for the changes between the raw and cooked potatoes. Make sure they understand that they should not attempt this activity without an adult.

Back at school
See if the children enjoyed their potato nests and if they had fun making them. Share some of the filling ideas. Can anybody tell you some of the differences between the raw and the cooked potato?

p105 Look for steam — FINDING OUT

Learning objective
- To know that water turns to steam when it is heated, but the steam turns back to water when it is cooled.

Lesson context
Working safely, boil a kettle to show how steam forms when water is heated. Hold a cold metal plate or tray over the steam to demonstrate that the steam turns back into water when it is cooled.

Setting the homework
Hand out the worksheets to the children and explain that they should look all round their home, inside and out, for sources of steam. Remind them that steam is hot and can be very dangerous.

Back at school
Where did the children find steam? Did they see any outside? Did anyone see evidence of steam cooling and condensing (for example, on a bathroom window)? Can they tell you why this happened?

p106 Cool it! — SCIENCE TO SHARE

Learning objective
- To know that some materials change when they are cooled.

Lesson context
In small groups, encourage the children to make ice cubes, and talk about how water changes from a liquid to a solid as it freezes. Talk about whether this change can be reversed and how we might go about this.

Setting the homework
Helpers may need advance warning of this activity in order to buy lemon meringue mix. Make sure the children know that they should look for changes in the lemon mixture as it cools.

Back at school
Ask the children what they noticed as the lemon mixture cooled (some could read what they have written on their sheet to the rest of the class). Did they enjoy making the pie?

p107 Cheese on toast — OBSERVATION

Learning objective
- To know that some materials melt and change when they are heated.

Lesson context
Ask the children to predict, and then find out, what happens to ice cubes when they are taken from the freezer and kept in a warm room. Ask them to observe closely the changes over time, noting that the ice cubes are changing back into water (from a solid to a liquid).

Setting the homework
Read through the sheet with the children. Make sure that they understand what to do, and that they should never use the toaster or grill without their helper.

Back at school
Ask the children if they enjoyed making their cheese on toast.. Did any of them try extra toppings? Was there a favourite? Ask some children to describe how the toast and cheese changed when they were heated.

p108 Hot spots — FINDING OUT

Learning objective
- To know that heat is a form of energy and that it may be supplied by several sources.

Lesson context
Talk about when, where and why we use heat. (To keep us warm, to cook food, and to iron with, for example.) Talk about some household appliances and think about what supplies the heat energy to each one (usually electricity or gas). Think about what it would be like living without any form of heat energy.

Setting the homework
Recap some of the heat sources you have talked about and where they get their energy from. Tell the children that they should look at home for as many heat sources as they can find, and decide from where they get their energy.

Back at school
Ask some of the children to read their lists. Ask: *Did anyone find anything different? Were there any unusual things?*

UNIT 5 ELECTRICITY MAKING CIRCUITS

p109 How many ways? — FINDING OUT

Learning objectives
- To know that electricity is used in many different ways.
- To know that mains electricity can be very dangerous and must be treated with extreme care.

Lesson context
Revise the electricity safety rules that the children learned in Year 1/Primary 2. Take the class on a walk around the school looking for the different ways in which electricity is used, and record uses of electricity in the classroom on a plan. Can the children tell you if electricity is being used safely in school?

Setting the homework
Name some devices that use electricity. Choose one and ask the children to tell you, in simple terms, what the electricity does and what we use it for (an iron, for example, is heated by electricity, and we use it to smooth our clothes). Encourage the children to give answers other than *It makes it work*.

Back at school
Look at some of the children's lists. Do any other children have different devices on their list?

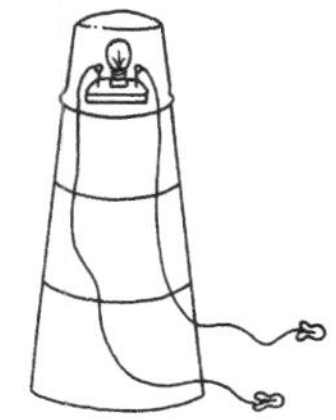

p110 Safety first — SCIENCE PRACTICE

Learning objective
- To know that mains electricity can be very dangerous and must be treated with extreme care.

Lesson context
Recap on the dangers of electricity, outdoors as well as indoors. Look at pictures of railway lines, pylons, sub-stations and so on and talk about the dangers of playing near them. Discuss the dangers of using electrical appliances near water.

Setting the homework
Hand out the worksheets and explain what the children have to do.

Back at school
Look at some of the children's posters and talk about the dangers they have included. The posters could then make a class display, or the children could take them back home and put them on their bedroom wall.

p111 What uses batteries? — SCIENCE TO SHARE

Learning objective
- To know that electricity can be supplied by batteries (cells).

Lesson context
Look at a selection of battery-operated devices (radios, clocks and so on). Try to operate them with and without batteries, to show the children that the battery supplies the electricity to make the objects work. Show the children a variety of different-sized batteries and practise inserting them into the devices to make them work.

Setting the homework
Explain the sheet to the children. Remind them that any equipment should be switched off and unplugged before they look for the batteries.

Back at school
Find out how many battery-operated devices the children found. Did they all use the same type of battery? What different types of battery are there?

p112 Complete the circuit — SCIENCE PRACTICE

Learning objectives
- To know that a complete circuit is needed for a device to work.
- To know the names of the components needed for a circuit to make a bulb light.

Lesson context
Show the children a simple circuit that makes a bulb light, and help the children to name each component. Break the circuit in various places and discuss what is needed to make the bulb light, reinforcing the idea that a complete circuit is always needed for the bulb to light. Draw and label a simple circuit on a board or flip chart.

Setting the homework
Explain the sheet with the children, making sure that they recognise each picture.

Back at school
Prepare a large copy of the sheet and, with the children, draw in the missing component and write its name in the box. Children can mark their own sheets as you do this.

UNIT 6 FORCES & MOTION | MAKING THINGS MOVE

p113 Pull or push? — SCIENCE PRACTICE

Learning objective

- To know that forces make things move.

Lesson context

Let the children experience moving wheeled toys or other objects around the classroom using a push or pull. Throw a ball up in the air, and describe the forces used (the push up, and the pull of gravity back down).

Setting the homework

Explain the sheet to the children and make sure they know what the pictures represent.

Back at school

Mark the sheets with the children. Pictures 1, 2, 6, 7 and 9 are pulls; the others are pushes.

p114 Push, pull or twist? — SCIENCE PRACTICE

Learning objective

- To know that actions such as stretching, squeezing, squashing, twisting and turning can be explained as forces (pushes and pulls).

Lesson context

Show the children, and allow them to see for themselves, a variety of actions that relate to forces, such as stretching fabrics and elastics, squashing play dough and sponges, or twisting the lid off a jar.

Setting the homework

Explain the sheet to the children. Ask for one or two examples of stretching, squeezing, squashing, twisting and turning to start them off.

Back at school

Share some of the children's drawings with the rest of the class. Check that the children have identified the forces in their pictures correctly.

p115 Forces wordsearch — LITERACY LINK

Learning objective

- To know that there is a force of friction between two surfaces.

Lesson context

Ask the children to rub their hands together and feel them getting warm. Explain that this is the force of friction. Look at how a bicycle wheel slows down as brakes are applied, and investigate friction by pulling a brick over different surfaces to see which surface requires the greatest pull.

Setting the homework

Read the words at the top of the sheet with the children and explain that they will be able to find all these words in the wordsearch. Help them to find the first word, if you feel it is appropriate.

Back at school

Check with the children to see who found all the words. Have they written the word *friction* in answer to the question? Did anyone make up their own wordsearch?

Answers:

		F	R	I	C	T	I	O	N
S	L	O	W	D	O	W	N		M
M									O
O	S	U	R	F	A	C	E		V
O					R				E
T					O		R		M
H	S	T	O	P	U		U		E
					G		B		N
					H				T

p116 Speeding up, slowing down — OBSERVATION

Learning objective

- To know that forces can make moving objects go faster, change direction or slow down.

Lesson context

Use PE equipment (bats and balls) to find out more about how forces speed things up, slow them down and make them change direction. Discuss what is happening, what forces are being used (pushes and pulls) and what other forces are acting (friction).

Setting the homework

Tell the children that, with their helper, they should look for examples of forces speeding things up, slowing them down or making them change direction. Ask them to think about what is happening and explain it to their helper.

Back at school

Ask the children to share some of the things they saw with the rest of the class. Read some of their sentences explaining why things speeded up, slowed down or changed direction.

p117 Sinking bottles — NUMERACY LINK

Learning objective

- To know that some objects float because water pushes up on them.

Lesson context

Remind the children of the work they did in Year 1/Primary 2, when they tried to push a ball under water. Float some margarine tub boats in a tank of water and load them with small objects until they sink. Discuss what is happening, and explain that when the boat floats, the upthrust of the water is greater than the force of gravity; when the boats are sufficiently loaded, gravity is greater and the boat sinks.

Setting the homework

Make sure that the children understand that they should not use glass bottles for this activity and they should have an adult with them. Remind them of the vocabulary they have learned and to think about these words when doing the activity.

Back at school

Look at the children's completed sheets. Can they explain what was happening? Can anyone tell you the word for the upward force of the water?

p118 All lit up — SCIENCE PRACTICE

Learning objective
- To know that light sources are used in different ways.

Lesson context
Ask the children to name some sources of light, and make a class list of their suggestions. Include the Sun and the stars in the list. Talk about how and when we use light, and distinguish between useful and purely decorative lights (such as Christmas tree lights). Think also about old-fashioned light sources such as gas and oil lamps.

Setting the homework
Explain the worksheet to the children. Ask them to bring the sheet back to school when they have finished.

Back at school
Look at some of the children's completed worksheets. What unusual light sources have the children found?

p119 Shadows — SCIENCE TO SHARE

Learning objective
- To know that light cannot pass through some materials and that is how shadows are created.

Lesson context
Take the children out to the playground to look at their shadows. See if they can catch or run away from them. Talk about where shadows falls relative to the Sun. In the classroom, ask pairs to draw silhouettes of one another.

Setting the homework
Explain the sheet to the children. Make sure they know that they should not move table lamps without their helper.

Back at school
What objects did the children use to make shadows? Share some of the pictures with the class – can the children guess what the objects were? What does opaque mean?

p120 Transparent, translucent, opaque — SCIENCE PRACTICE

Learning objective
- To know that light can pass through some materials, but not others.

Lesson context
Test a collection of different materials (for example, plastics, wood, pottery and fabrics) to find out whether they are transparent, translucent or opaque by placing them over a black-and-white picture and asking the children whether they can see the image through the picture. Sort the materials into groups based on their findings and talk about where each would be useful.

Setting the homework
Recap the vocabulary with the children and ask them if they can tell you what each word means. Tell them that they are going to look for things at home to put into each group.

Back at school
Prepare an enlarged copy of the worksheet and write in the names of some of the objects or materials that the children have found. Which group was it easiest to find things for? Define the vocabulary again for the children.

p121 Solar energy — FINDING OUT

Learning objective
- To know that light is a form of energy.

Lesson context
Talk about electricity as a form of energy that makes things work. Look at a torch with and without batteries, and discuss how it works. Show the children a solar-powered calculator and explain that it uses light (solar) energy to make it work. Remind the children that plants use light energy to make their food.

Setting the homework
Explain the worksheet to the children. Remind them that they will need to look in books (either from home or the library), use the Internet or ask an adult. See if they can think of a few examples to start them off.

Back at school
Make a big picture of the Sun and write the names of the things that the children found out about on the picture.

p122 Sounds at home — LITERACY LINK

Learning objective
- To know that we use sounds in a variety of ways.

Lesson context
Ask the children to close their eyes and to listen carefully to the sounds around the classroom. Can they tell what is happening from just the sounds they hear? How? Role-play telephone conversations and revise making an emergency call from Year 1/Primary 2. Talk about some other sounds we might hear during the day and what they might tell us. Remind the children that some sounds may give us pleasure, such as music.

Setting the homework
Explain the sheet to the children, and tell them that it might be easier to note sounds down as they hear them, rather than trying to remember them.

Back at school
Choose some children to talk about the sounds they heard, and ask others to read what they have written. Which sound was heard most often? Do the class have a favourite sound?

p123 Warning sounds — OBSERVATION

Learning objective
- To know that sounds can act as warnings.

Lesson context
Ask the children to think about sounds they hear during the day. Do any of them give a warning of some kind? Talk about sounds that should never be ignored, such as ambulance sirens, pedestrian crossings and lorries reversing. Discuss other sorts of warning sounds, like telephones, shop bells, oven timers and so on. If possible, practise responding to the fire bell.

Setting the homework
This homework will need a week to complete. Read through the sheet with the children and make sure they understand what they have to do.

Back at school
Share some of the children's lists. *Can anybody say which sounds warn of danger and which do not? Can anyone tell me what we should do if we hear the fire bell?*

p124 Making sounds — SCIENCE TO SHARE

Learning objective

- To know how to make a range of sounds using a collection of materials and objects.

Lesson context

Ask the children to make simple musical instruments from a collection of recycled materials, then play a tune with them.

Setting the homework

Read through the sheet together and make sure the children know how to code their 'instrument' selection in order to write their rhythms or tunes. Tell them that if they are able to record their tunes you will play them back at school.

Back at school

Ask the children if they had fun making up tunes. Play any tapes they have brought in. Ask the class if they can guess what was used to make the sounds.

p125 Sound puzzle — LITERACY LINK

Learning objective

- To know that sounds get fainter as they travel away from a source and that loud sounds travel further than quiet sounds.

Lesson context

Carry out an experiment with the children to see how sounds get fainter the further away they are. Stand the children in a circle with a sound source in the centre. Ask them to walk away from the sound until they can no longer hear it, marking this position with a beanbag. Repeat the experiment, this time walking towards the sound until they can hear it – is there a difference between the two results?

Setting the homework

Hand out the worksheet. Tell the children that it will recap all the work they have been doing about sound. Make sure they know that they need to solve the crossword first.

Back at school

Check that the children solved the crossword correctly and managed to complete the sentences.

UNIT 8 EARTH & BEYOND — THE SUN AND THE SEASONS

p126 Sun diary — FINDING OUT

Learning objective

- To know that the Sun appears to move across the sky in a regular way.

Lesson context

Ask the children to make regular observations over the course of the day to notice the apparent movement of the Sun across the sky. Talk about the fact that it is actually the Earth rotating that makes the Sun appear to move.

Setting the homework

This homework is best done in the summer and will take a week to complete. Remind the children that they must never look directly at the Sun, and that they should choose an object that is in sunlight when the Sun is shining so that they can observe the shadow.

Back at school

Ask the children if they noticed any change in the position of the shadow between the morning and the evening. Were they able to observe the shadows every day? Ask: *Can you explain why the shadow moves?*

p127 The Moon in space — LITERACY LINK

Learning objective

- To know that we only see the Moon because it reflects light from the Sun.

Lesson context

Use a polystyrene ball and OHP to show that the Moon does not produce any light of its own, but that we see it because it reflects the light of the Sun.

Setting the homework

Read through the sheet with the children and explain that they are going to find out more about the Moon from books, the library and, perhaps, the Internet. Suggest that they could also ask an adult to see if they remember the first Moon landings. You may wish to allow several days for children to complete this homework.

Back at school

Read some of the completed sheets. Where did children find their information? Talk about some of the interesting thing they have added. How many were able to find out how much they would weigh on the Moon?

p128 Mapping the weather — SCIENCE TO SHARE

Learning objectives

- To use weather records to see the pattern of the seasons.
- To collect, present and interpret data.

Lesson context

Talk about why it is useful to know about weather patterns and how some people (such as farmers or skiers) use that knowledge. Talk about the differences between the seasons, and how weather records can tell us about changes in the pattern of the seasons. Ask groups to interpret weather data and find out about seasonal differences, using weather data from newspapers or the Internet.

Setting the homework

Has anybody seen the weather forecast on TV? Did they notice the symbols that were used? What do they mean? Ask the children to watch the weather forecast with their helper before they complete the sheet.

Back at school

What are some of the seasonal differences the children have shown on their maps? Can they tell you the main differences between winter and summer? Are autumn and spring as different from each other as winter and summer?

Name:

Getting dressed

- Fill in the spaces to complete the labels.
- Use the words in the box to help you.

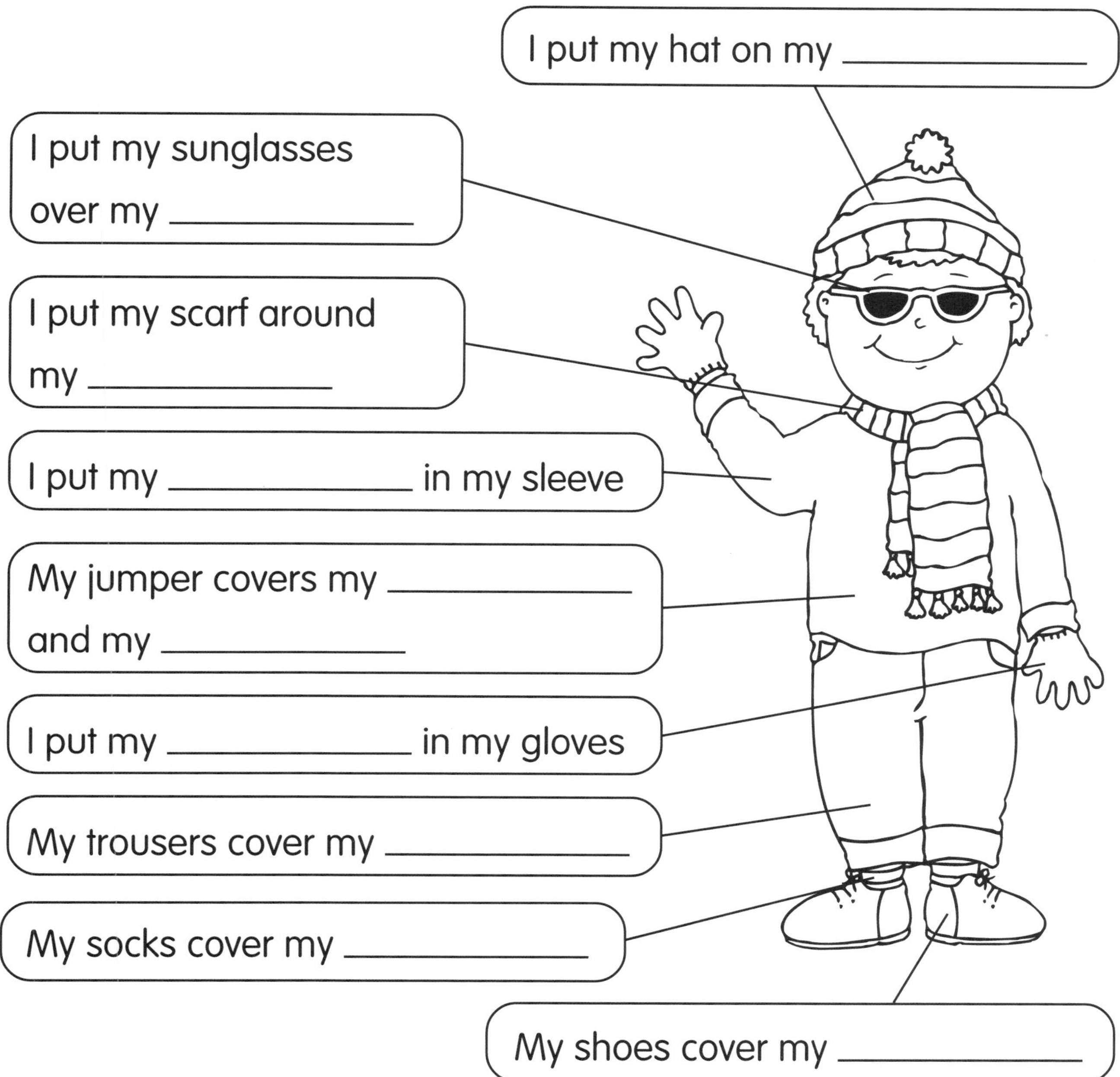

I put my hat on my ____________
I put my sunglasses over my ____________
I put my scarf around my ____________
I put my ____________ in my sleeve
My jumper covers my ____________ and my ____________
I put my ____________ in my gloves
My trousers cover my ____________
My socks cover my ____________
My shoes cover my ____________

head	**hands**	**feet**	**arms**	**legs**
arm	**chest**	**neck**	**eyes**	**feet**

Dear Helper,

This activity will help your child learn and remember the names of parts of their body. If necessary, help them to read the labels and the list of words in the box, and offer help writing the labels. As they complete the sheet, ask them to point to the correct parts of themselves. Challenge your child by asking them to name and point to as many other parts of their bodies as they can. For example, can they name the different parts that make up a leg (knee, thigh, calf, ankle, shin)?

Name:

Name the senses

- Colour in the pictures, then write the name of the sense underneath it.

smell **touch** **taste** **hear** **see**

Dear Helper,

We use our senses to find out about our world and everything in it. Children need to be helped to develop these senses; encourage your child to tell you which senses they are using as they go about their everyday activities. Describing what they smell, touch, taste, hear and see will help them to develop their language skills.

Name:

Let's go round the mulberry bush

- Play 'Here we go round the mulberry bush'.
- See if you can include the following actions:

This is the way we stamp our feet	This is the way we sit on the floor
This is the way we clap our hands	This is the way we nod our heads
This is the way we bend our knees	This is the way we wave our hands

- Draw pictures of yourself doing the actions in the boxes.
- Play the game again, this time with your own verses.

Dear Helper,

Playing this game and talking about it will help your child to identify some of the ways in which their body moves. Your child has played this game at school and should know the tune already. Talk about the ways in which their body moves and practise some of the new words they have learned, such as *walk, run, jump, skip, hop, stretch* and *crawl*. See if your child can name the parts of their body they are using for each movement, in particular the joints (for example, hip, knee, ankle, shoulder, elbow and wrist).

Name:

Me growing up

- Look at some photographs of yourself growing up and draw some pictures below.

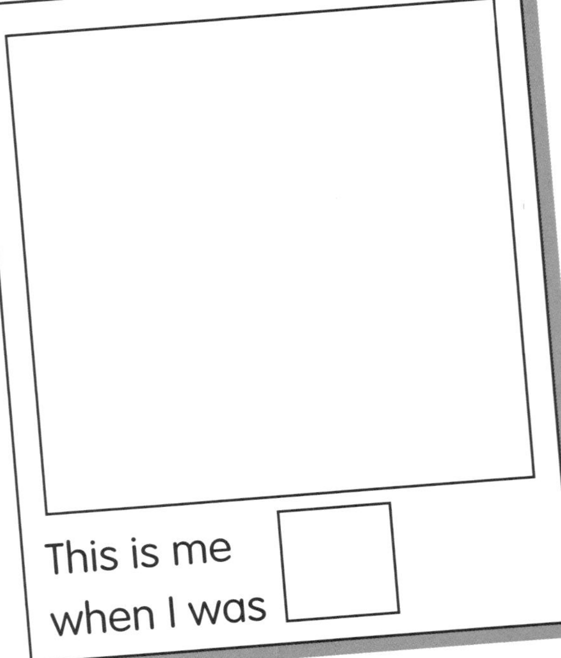

This is me when I was

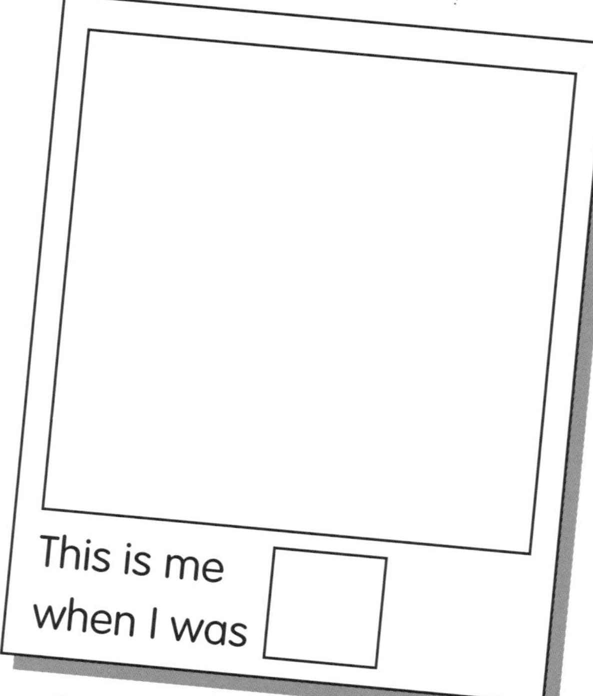

This is me when I was

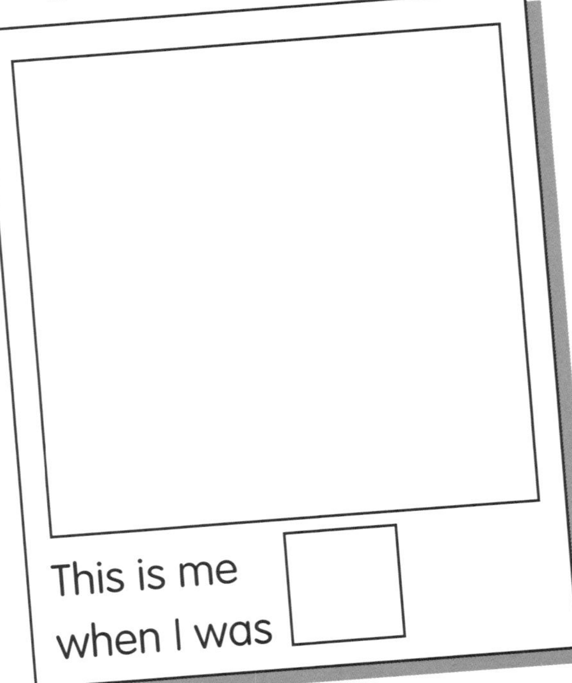

This is me when I was

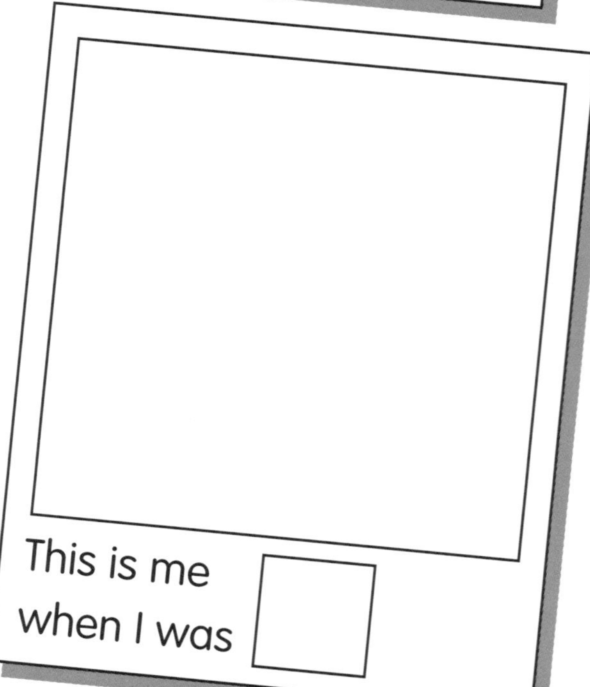

This is me when I was

Dear Helper,

If possible, look at some family photographs showing your child at different ages to help them see how they have grown. Look at them together and talk about how they have changed from when they were born until now. Discuss some of the things they couldn't do as a baby but find quite easy now (such as having a bath or eating). If you don't have any photographs available, talk about what your child was like as a baby and as a toddler and encourage them to draw pictures.

Name:

My family

- Draw a picture of your family, including each member.
- Put the youngest at one end and the oldest at the other.
- Find out how old each person is and write under their picture.

Dear Helper,

Help your child to make a list of all the members of their immediate family, from the youngest to the oldest (including grandfathers and grandmothers). If you have photographs available, look at them together. Point out the differences between the generations to help them identify the different stages in the human life cycle (baby, child, teenager, young adult, middle life and old age). Although there will not be room to draw them all on the sheet, you could extend this activity by making a list of other family members including uncles, aunts, cousins and so on. Help your child to order these from youngest to oldest, which will help develop their numeracy skills.

Name:

Shopping for food and drink

- Draw and label some of the foods you bought at the shop.

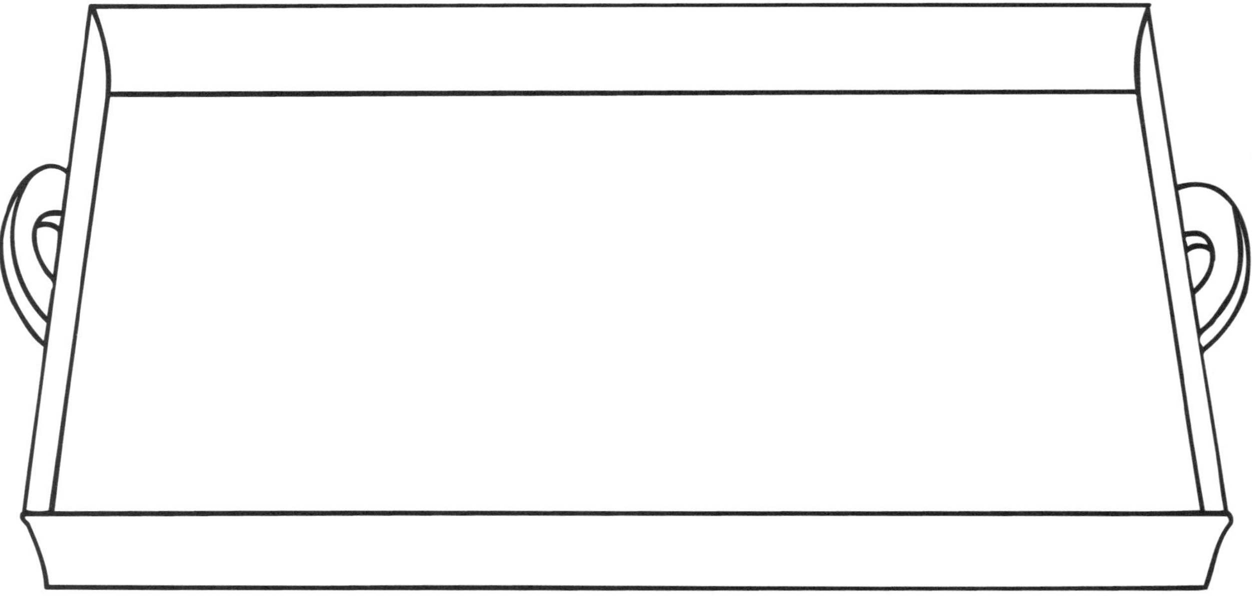

- Draw and label some of the drinks you bought at the shop.

- Complete this sentence:

We need ______________________ and ______________________ in order to stay alive and healthy.

Dear Helper,

If it's possible, take your child shopping with you, or let them help to unpack the shopping. If you have time, let them sort the food and drink into different groups before putting it away. Talk about how food and water are essential for staying alive and keeping healthy, and about the fact that our liquid intake is often in the form of soft drinks, tea or coffee and so on. See if they can complete the sentence with *food* and *water*.

Name:

UNIT 2 ANIMALS & PLANTS GROWING AND CARING

Dead or alive?

- Find and draw some things that are:

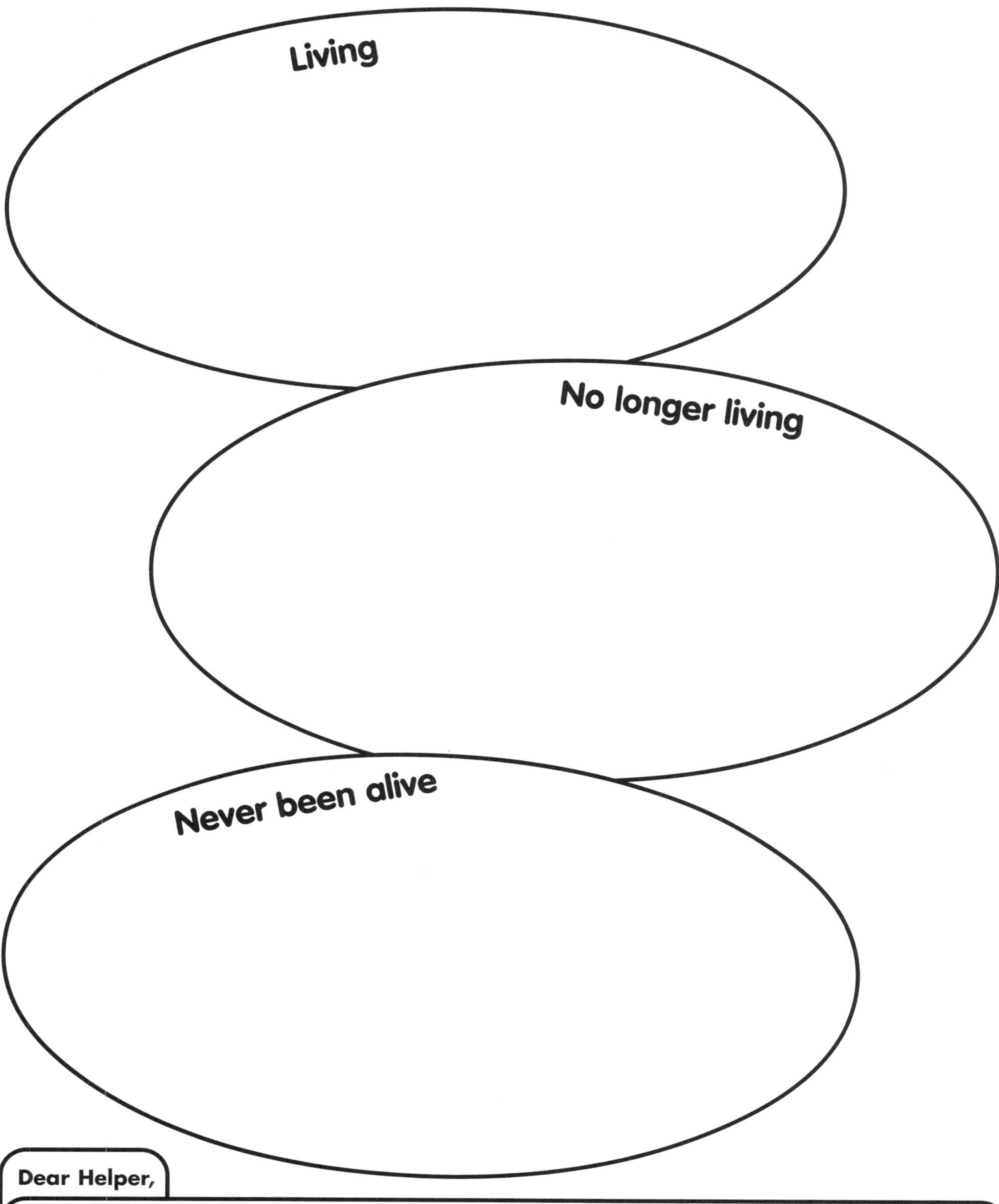

Dear Helper,

Children can often distinguish between things that are alive and things that are dead. However, they sometimes get confused when it comes to distinguishing between things that are dead and those that have never been alive, such as between a wooden spoon and a stone (a wooden spoon was once part of a living tree, but a stone has always been a stone). This activity will help your child to understand the differences between each group. Encourage them to look around the house and garden, noting some of the things they find that fit into each category.

PHOTOCOPIABLE

Name:

What is it?

- Fill in the blank spaces with either the animal's name or a picture.

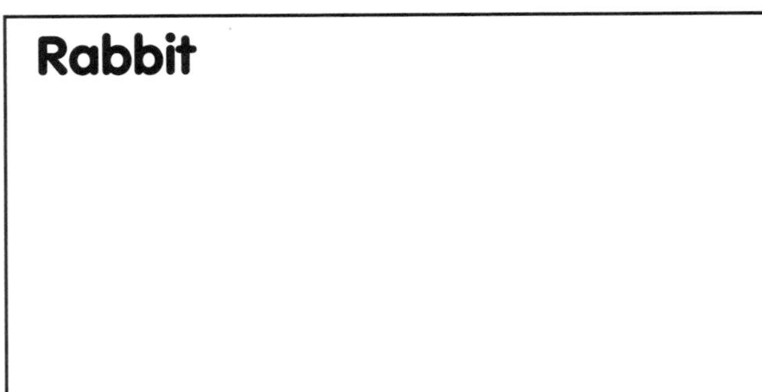

Rabbit

Dog

- Draw your favourite animal on the back of the sheet.

Dear Helper,

These animals should be familiar to your child, as they have been looking at different animals in class. For each animal, encourage your child to talk about the things that help them to identify it (for example, the swan has a long neck; the cow has udders). If you are out with your child and see any animals, play the 'Recognise and name' game with them. Challenge your child to name unfamiliar animals they may see in books or on TV.

Name:

Beetle

You will need: a dice and shaker, pencils, paper for other players.

- Two or more people can play this game.
- Throw a 6 to start by drawing a body (you only need one of these).
- Throw a 5 to draw a head (you only need one of these).
- Throw a 4 for each wing (you need two of these).
- Throw a 3 for each eye (you need two of these).
- Throw a 2 for each antenna (you need two of these).
- Throw a 1 for each leg (you need six of these).

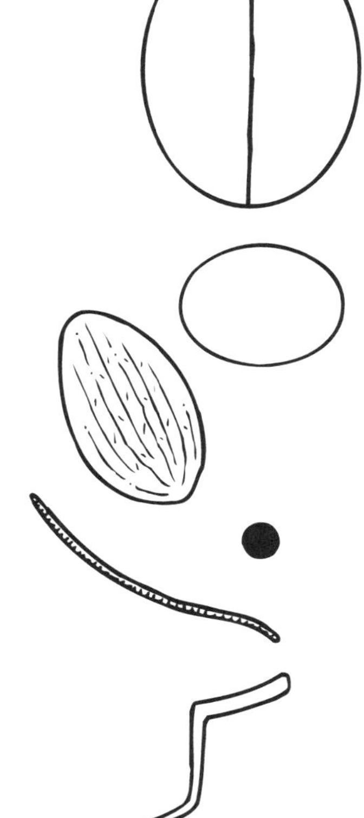

- The winner is the first person to make a complete beetle. Draw your beetle parts in the space below as you throw the dice.

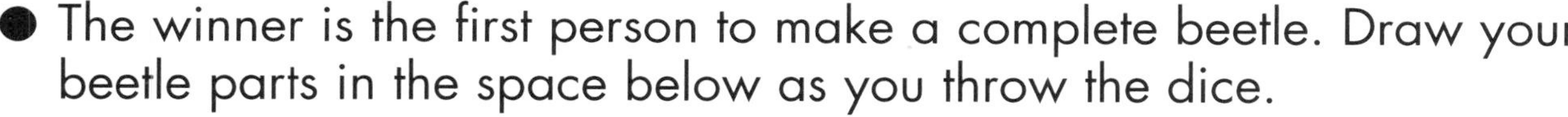

Dear Helper,

This is a fun game that everybody can play which will help your child to recognise and name some of the main external parts of a small creature. Players take it in turns to throw the dice and draw the appropriate part of the beetle if it's still required. You must throw a six and draw a body to start. The winner is the first person to complete their beetle. Let your child draw their beetle on this sheet to take back to school; other players will need a piece of paper each on which to draw their creature. Extend this activity by making up your own game based on a different animal (for example, an elephant, including trunk and tusks).

Name:

How do they move?

- Look for animals when you are out and about.
- Look at them carefully and watch how they move.
- Write their names on the sheet and describe how they move.
- Ask your helper to help you with the writing.

Name of animal	How does it move?
slug	*It slides along the ground. It hasn't got any legs but its underneath is called a foot.*

Dear Helper,

Your child is learning about how animals move and comparing their movements to the ways in which humans move. When looking for animals, encourage your child to compare the movements of any animals you see with their own movements, noting both similarities and differences. For example, a human and a dog can both run but one uses two legs and the other four. Look for as wide a variety of animals as possible such as cats, birds, butterflies, caterpillars, horses and so on. If your child has difficulty writing everything they want to note, write down their words for them.

Name:

I-spy plants

- Look for these plants on your way home or when you are out.
- Colour each one when you have seen it.

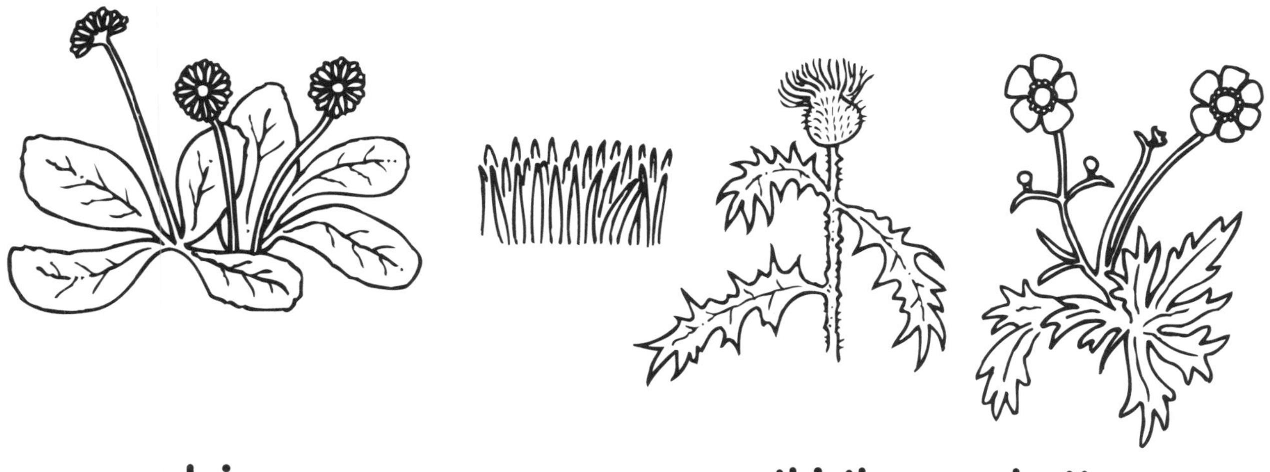

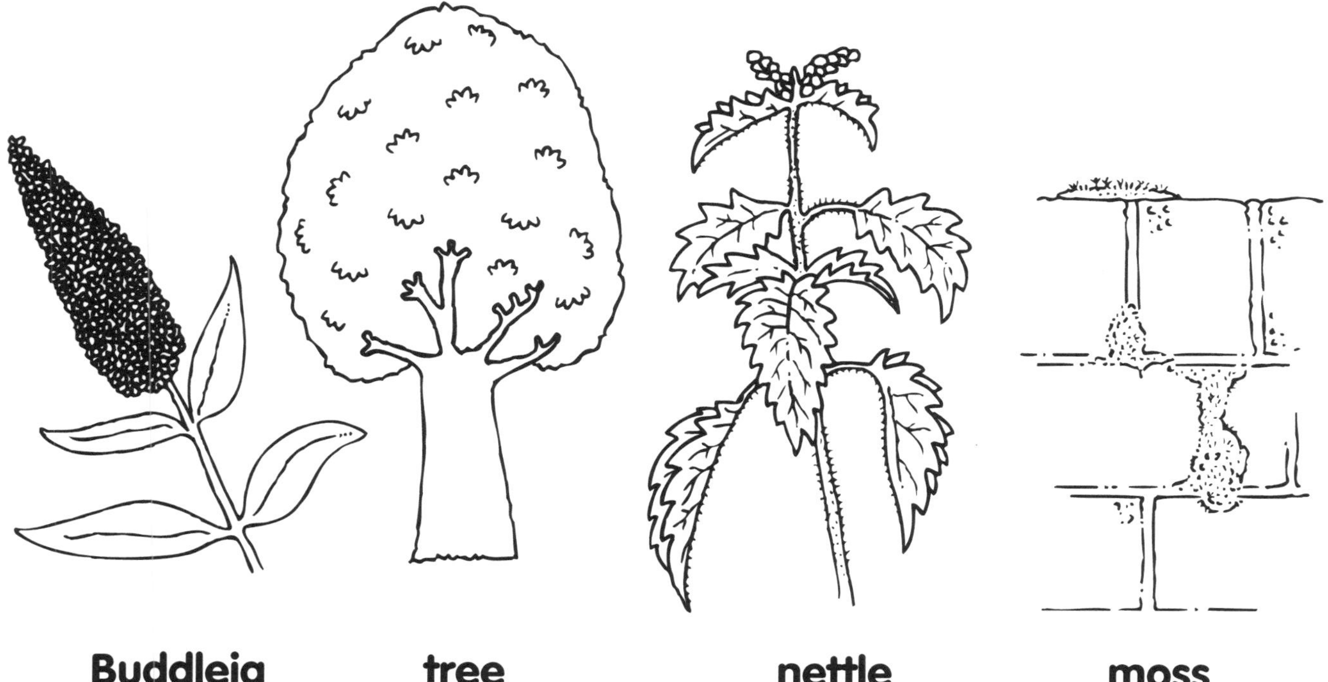

Dear Helper,

This simple game will help your child to recognise and learn the names of some common plants. You may not find all the plants listed in your area, but if you wish your child could draw, colour and label one or two plants that are not listed on the back of the sheet. Challenge your child to find out what type of tree they have seen (your local library will have reference books to help).

Name:

Growing seeds is fun

You will need: a plant pot or yoghurt pot with a hole in the bottom for drainage, some seeds, and compost or soil to fill the pot.

- You can grow your own plants from seeds.
- Plant the seeds carefully with your helper, look after them and watch them grow.
- You will need to be patient!
- Write about what you did.

What kind of seeds did you plant?

____

____

How did you plant them?

____

____

____

What do you need to do to care for them?

____

____

____

Dear Helper,

Save the seeds from any fruit your child might eat (orange, lemon and grapefruit seeds usually germinate well or use the seeds from peppers or melons). Set them in a pot of compost. Plant several seeds to make sure you get at least one to germinate, then remove all but the strongest seedling once they start to grow. Encourage your child to care for the plant, watering it regularly (but not too much!), and observe any changes as it grows. Talk about how the plants that they eat grow from seeds.

Name:

Info

Sort the tins

- Make sure you ask before you open any cupboards at home.
- Look at the tins of food in the kitchen cupboard.
- Sort out the tins containing food that comes from plants.
- Make a list of all those you find.

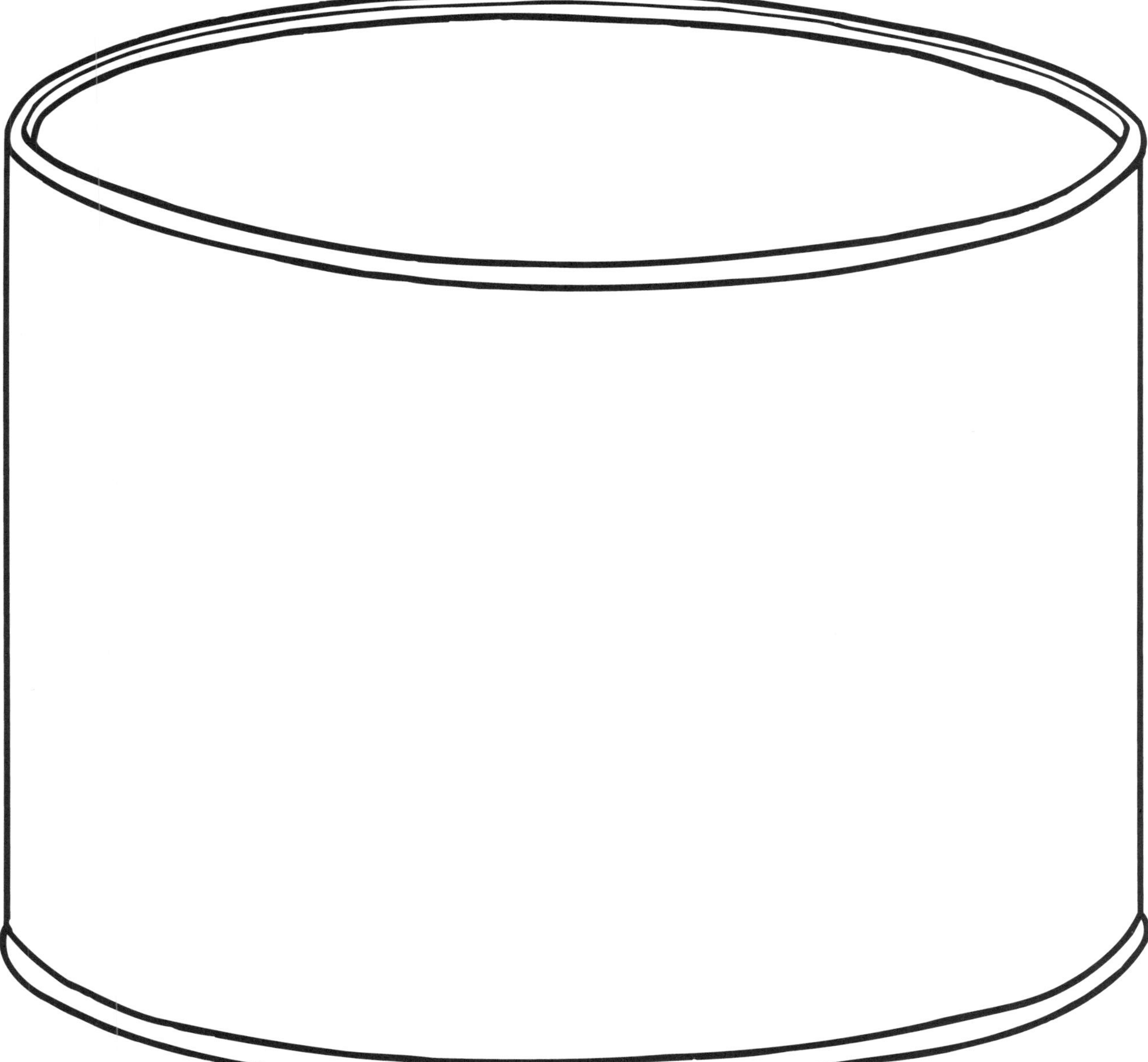

Dear Helper,

Look through the kitchen cupboard together and read the labels on the tins. Decide which contain food made from plants. Discuss foods such as spaghetti and help your child understand that it is made from flour that comes from a plant. Some tins may contain foods from plants and animals (for example, chicken and mushroom soup) – talk about whether or not you should include these tins in your list. To extend the activity, try reading the list of ingredients on each tin to see if your child can describe the type of plant the food comes from. For example, peaches grow on a tree and rice is a type of grass. This will help your child learn that plants provide a wide range of foods.

Name:

Salad for tea

- Think of the some of the things you might put in a salad for tea.
- Draw and label pictures of the things you would put in your favourite salad.

- Perhaps you could help to make a salad for tea.

Dear Helper,

Talk about the different things you might put in a salad to help your child appreciate that fruit and vegetables are an important part of a balanced diet. Help your child to write the labels if necessary. Encourage your child to help prepare whatever kind of salad your family enjoys – rice, pasta, green or fruit, for example. Show them how to use a knife safely. If they are cutting fruit or vegetables they will need a suitable sharp knife; using a blunt knife can be equally dangerous (and more frustrating), since more pressure is used to try and cut the food, which can result in trapped and badly bruised fingers.

Name:

Weather record

- Draw a picture to show what the weather is like each morning and evening.

	Morning	Evening
Monday		
Tuesday		
Wednesday		
Thursday		
Friday		
Saturday		
Sunday		

Dear Helper,

Help your child to remember to check the weather each day before and after school, drawing the appropriate picture in the space on the table. This will help develop your child's skills of observation, and also to appreciate the range of weather we have in this country and the effect it has on our daily lives. After school, talk about whether the weather is the same now as it was in the morning. For example, it may have been sunny in the morning, but raining by the end of school.

Name:

Blowing in the wind

- Take your wind meter home with you.
- Explain to your helper how it works.
- Use it to measure the strength of the wind each day when you get home from school.
- Colour in the number of strips that are blowing each day.

Monday				
Tuesday				
Wednesday				
Thursday				
Friday				
Saturday				
Sunday				

Dear Helper,

Your child has made a simple wind meter at school. It has streamers of different weights that will blow in the wind. The lightest one will blow in a gentle breeze, but only a stronger wind will move the heavier ones. Help your child to 'measure' the wind each day when they come home from school by noting the number of streamers that are moving, and recording this on the sheet. This will develop your child's understanding that the strength of the wind changes. It will also help to develop their skills of observation. Challenge your child to find out the direction from which the wind is blowing.

Name:

Signs of the seasons – autumn

What season is it? ____________________

- Go for a walk with your helper and see how many different kinds of fruit you can find.
- Draw pictures of those that you find and label the ones you know the names of.
- Remember, never eat any seeds or berries unless an adult tells you it is safe to do so.

Dear Helper,

This activity will help your child learn about some of the things they might find in the autumn. On your walk, you may find seed heads, berries and other fruits in the garden or in the local environment. Look for rose hips, acorns, horse chestnuts, and for the ripening seed heads on bedding plants and other flowers. Talk about how they all contain seeds or a seed that can grow into a new plant. If you find any seeds, your child could stick them onto the sheet with their drawings. You could also plant some seeds to help your child understand the cycle of growth.

Name:

Signs of the seasons – winter

What season is it? ______________________

- Look around your home, inside and out, and draw some of the things that tell you which season it is.

- Finish this sentence.

I know it is ____________________ because it was ______________

when I went to bed and ________________________ when I got up.

Dear Helper,

Learning about the seasons helps develop your child's sense of time as well as their awareness of seasonal changes in the weather and the environment. Help them to look for things they may not have noticed at school, asking questions such as: *Do we have doors and windows open in summer and closed in winter? How is the park or garden different from how it looked in the summer? Do we dress differently or play different games? Was it light or dark when you went to bed and got up in the morning?* If necessary, help them to choose the right words to complete the sentence.

Name:

Signs of the seasons – spring

What season is it? ______________________

- Colour the picture and put a circle round all the things you can see that tell you it is spring.
- Add something else to the picture that you might see in the spring.

Dear Helper,

When you are out and about with your child, look for changes that happen in spring and talk about them. Look for blossom on trees, new shoots coming through, birds collecting nesting materials and so on. Ask: *Why do you think these things are happening?* (The weather is getting warmer and the days are getting longer, so plants are beginning to grow. Animals have their babies in spring, when food is plentiful, so that there is time for them to grow and get fat before the winter sets in.)

Name:

Signs of the seasons – summer

What season is it? ______________________

- Which pictures are the odd ones out? Put a cross through them.
- Colour all the pictures that you would find in summer.

I know it is ____________________ because ____________________

Dear Helper,

Learning about the seasons helps develop your child's awareness of the seasonal changes in the weather and the environment. Look at the pictures above with them and decide which of the pictures they are least likely to find in the summer. Help them to complete the sentence to explain how they know it is summer. (The odd pictures out are: the daffodil, the long shadow, the snowman, the acorn, the winter clothes.)

Name:

I-spy minibeasts

- Go out on a minibeast safari.
- Tick the ones you see.

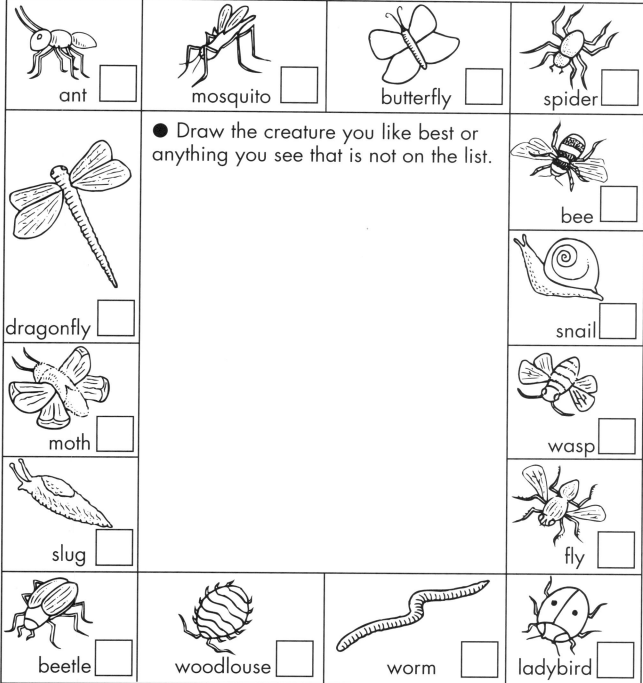

ant ☐	mosquito ☐	butterfly ☐	spider ☐
dragonfly ☐	• Draw the creature you like best or anything you see that is not on the list.		bee ☐
			snail ☐
moth ☐			wasp ☐
slug ☐			fly ☐
beetle ☐	woodlouse ☐	worm ☐	ladybird ☐

Dear Helper,

Your child has been learning the names of some common creatures, or minibeasts, and this activity will help to reinforce these names and develop their observation skills. Together, go out on a minibeast safari in your garden, a park, the countryside or a churchyard, and help your child to appreciate the variety of living things. Tick off each creature as you see it (you may have more than one tick in each box). Extend the activity by looking at books on different creatures from the library and talking about how, for example, there are many different types of spider and not just one.

Name:

Feed the birds

- Make a bird feeder like the one in the picture.

You will need: a medium-sized soft drinks bottle, a length of string, some sticky tape (insulating tape is best), sharp scissors and a bradawl (for adult use), some bird food (seeds or crumbs).

You will need an adult to help you

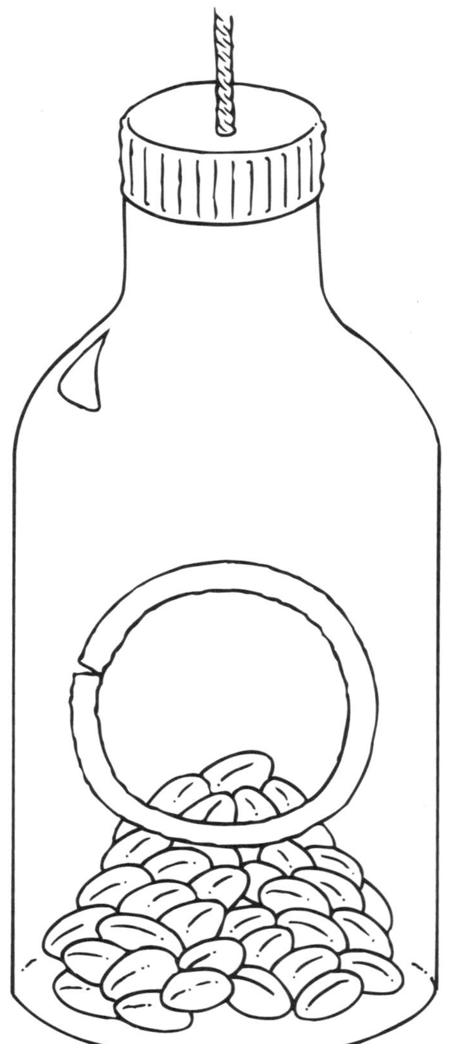

What to do:

1. Cut a hole in the side of the bottle about 6cm across.

2. Cover any sharp edges with sticky tape.

3. Pierce a hole in the lid using the bradawl.

4. Thread a piece of string through the hole and tie a knot to stop the string slipping out.

5. Fill the bottle with bird food and hang it outside where it can easily be seen.

- Don't lose heart – sometimes it takes a while for birds to get used to a new feeder. Make a list of any birds you see.

Dear Helper,

Please make sure that only adults use the scissors and bradawl when making the bird feeder. Children need to learn the names of common animals, including birds. By making a bird feeder your child will learn that caring for other living creatures is important and can be fun. Help them to identify any birds that come to the feeder or any others you may see (early morning or late afternoon are good times to see garden birds). You may find it helpful to borrow a bird book from the local library to help you recognise some of the birds if they are unfamiliar to you.

Name:

My bedroom

- Your bedroom is your habitat.
- Draw a picture of it and everything in it.

Dear Helper,

Your child has been learning about different habitats within the environment. Their bedroom is their small habitat within the wider environment of the home. Encourage them to look around their bedroom and think about what makes it into their habitat. They should draw things they are particularly attached to and talk about how these things make their bedroom special.

Name:

What's it like?

- See if you can find some things with each of these properties.
- Draw a picture of it in the correct box.

hard	soft	flexible

rigid	opaque	transparent

Dear Helper,

Your child has been looking at the properties of different materials. Help them to look around the house for a wide range of materials – they may find more than one to go in each category. Some materials could perhaps go in more than one category, for example glass could go in both the hard and transparent categories; fabric might be classed as soft, flexible or opaque. Help your child to decide which category to put each material in, using the words in the boxes and making sure they understand what they mean.

Name:

What's it made from?

- Can you find something at home made from each of these materials?

- Draw pictures of the things you found and label them.

Dear Helper,

This activity will help your child's observation and writing skills. Look around the house together to find objects made from each of the materials listed above. Plastics can be made to mimic many different materials, so your child may need help to distinguish, for example, a clear glass bowl from a clear plastic one or a wooden table from a plastic one.

Name:

Is it magnetic?

You will need: a magnet or a small piece of magnetic tape.

- Use your magnet to find some things in your home that are magnetic and some that are not.
- Make a list or draw pictures in the space below.

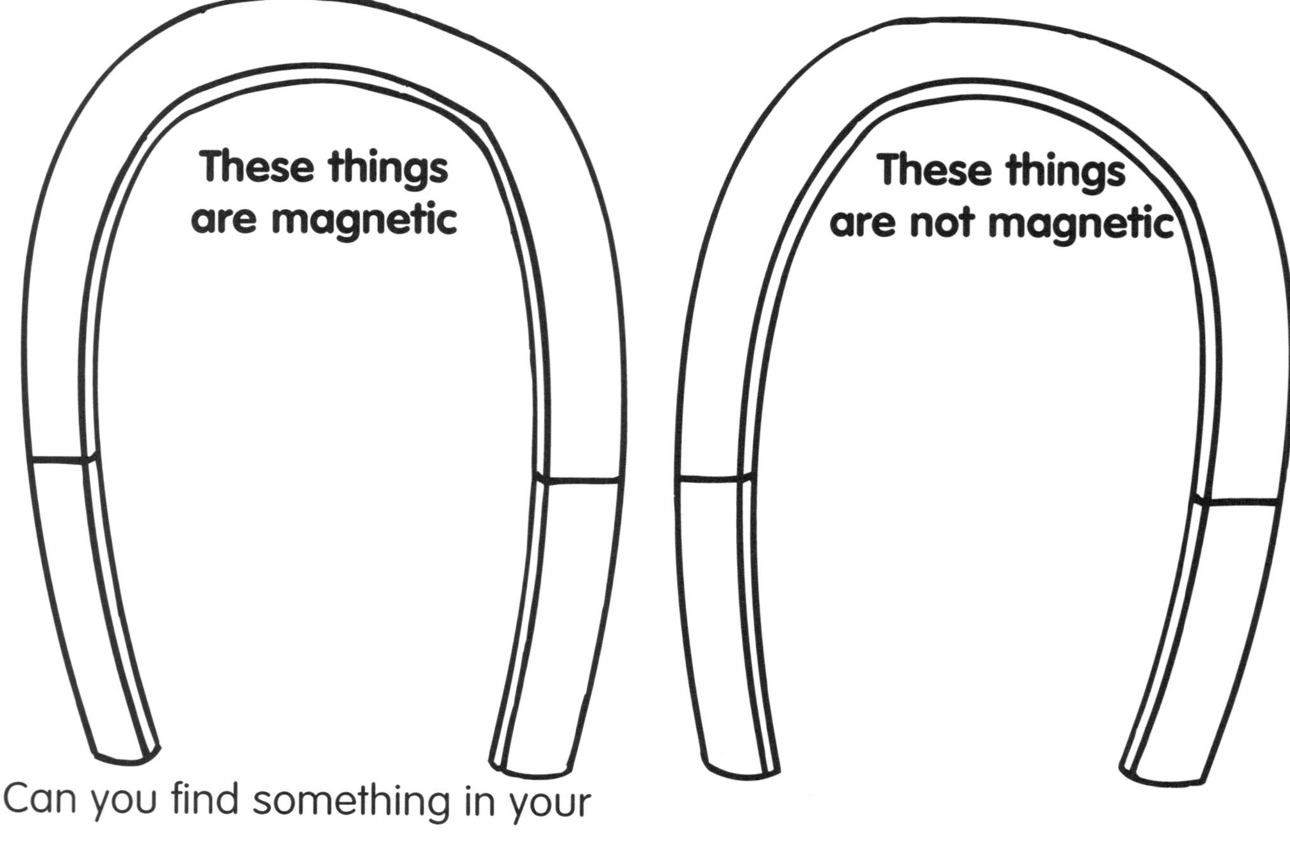

Can you find something in your house that uses magnets to work? ____________________

Think of something that you could do if you had a huge magnet.

____

____

Dear Helper,

Your child should have a small piece of magnetic tape to help them with this activity, although you could use a conventional magnet if you have one. Encourage them to test a variety of different materials around the home (it's important not to put magnets near TVs, tape recorders, telephones or computers as they can be damaged easily by them). When they have completed their lists, talk about how all the magnetic things are made from metal. There may be some metal things in the non-magnetic list, since metals such as brass, silver, gold and aluminium are not magnetic. For the last two questions, you may find kitchen cupboards or wardrobes that have magnetic catches, and encourage your child to imagine what they could do with a huge magnet.

Name:

More of the same

- Look around at home and find as many boxes or containers as you can. Are they all made from the same material?
- Draw some of them and write the name of the material they are made from underneath the picture.

- Can you find examples of these things that are made from different materials? Write the names of the materials next to each picture.

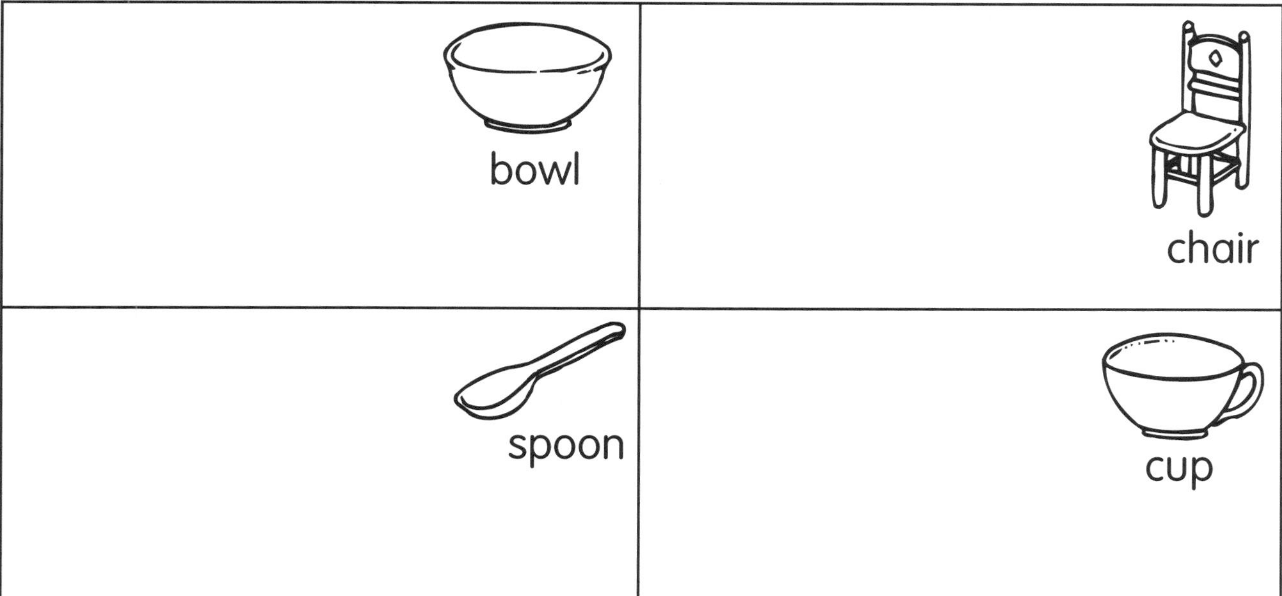

Dear Helper,

This activity will help your child appreciate the variety of materials that we use in everyday life, and that simple objects can be made from different materials. Objects may have the same basic function (for example, all boxes hold or store things), but they may be slightly different in terms of size or construction. Talk about why things are sometimes made from different materials: a shoebox need not be airtight so is made from card, but a cake tin needs to be airtight in order to keep the contents fresh, and is therefore made from metal or plastic.

Name:

How many things?

wood **metal** **plastic** **glass** **stone**

- Choose one of the materials listed above, and circle it.
- Find as many things that are made from that material as you can.
- Draw or write the name of everything you find in the boxes below.

Inside my house

Outside my house

Dear Helper,

Together, look around the inside and outside of the house for different things that are made from the same material. Plastic comes in many forms, so this may lead to some discussion about why it needs to be rigid (for boxes and buckets) or flexible (for bags and sheeting). Challenge your child to think about why a certain material may be used for different purposes depending on its properties, for example whether it is waterproof, transparent or rigid.

Name:

How many materials?

- Choose an object like a favourite toy that is made from lots of materials.
- Draw a picture of it and label the different materials used.

- You could use some of these words to help you write your labels.

metal **plastic** **fabric** **wood** **leather**
glass **stone** **clay** **paper** **card**

Dear Helper,

This activity will help develop your child's writing and observation skills. Many objects are made from more than one material, each being chosen for its particular properties. A baby buggy, for example, has a metal frame for strength, rubber tyres for a smooth ride, and a fabric seat for comfort. Encourage your child to explain why the different materials in their chosen object have been used to help them learn that materials are chosen for their properties.

Is it waterproof?

- Find three or four things that you think are waterproof.
- What do you think each one is made from?
- Test each one with your helper by pouring water over it or taking it in the bath with you.
- Fill in the chart.

My object is:	I think it is made from:	I found that it was ✔ was not ✘ waterproof

Dear Helper,

You may want to supervise this activity fairly closely (or at least the choosing of the objects to be tested!). Try to choose some objects that will and will not be waterproof (an umbrella and a jumper, for example). If it is fine outside, a jug of water and washing-up bowl is a good way to test the materials; otherwise, your child could test them in the bath. Discuss how not all materials are waterproof, and why some things do need to be waterproof, such as an umbrella, wellington boots, a cereal bowl and so on.

Name:

Egg sandwiches

You will need: an egg, a small saucepan filled with water, two slices of bread, butter or margarine, a knife and fork.

- Make some egg sandwiches for your tea.
- Here's what you need to do:

1. Choose an egg.
2. Put it carefully into a saucepan of cold water.
3. Put the pan on the cooker and ask an adult to help you turn it on.
4. Boil the egg for ten minutes.
5. Ask an adult to help you take it off the cooker.
6. Run cold water over the egg to cool it down.
7. Remove the shell and put the egg into a basin.

8. Add a small amount of butter or margarine (and some salad cream if you like it) and chop up the egg using a fork.
9. Spread some butter on two slices of bread and spread the mixture onto one of the slices.
10. Put the other slice of bread on top, cut it into four and enjoy your egg sandwich!

- Draw a picture of yourself enjoying your egg sandwiches.

Dear Helper,

Your child has been looking at changing objects using forces in class. This is a good activity to do together, but encourage your child to read and follow the instructions themselves, just giving help where necessary. They could tick off or highlight each instruction as they do it to help them follow the recipe. As they are making the sandwiches, talk about how they are using a pushing force to chop (change the shape of) the egg, to spread the mixture and to cut the sandwiches.

Name:

Electrical things

Don't touch anything that uses electricity!

- Look around your home and find some things that use mains electricity.
- Draw pictures of the things you find in each room.

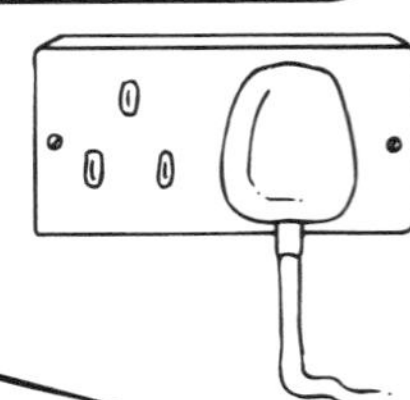

Dear Helper,

Your child has been learning about electricity at school. Together, look around the house for things that use mains electricity, including less obvious items such as a fridge or central heating. Your child has also been learning about the dangers of electricity. Talk about why there are usually no electrical things in the bathroom. Emphasise the dangers of mixing mains electricity with water.

Name:

UNIT 5 ELECTRICITY USING AND MISUSING ELECTRICITY

Batteries

- Look around your home and see how many things you can find that use batteries.
- Draw pictures of the things you find.

- Write the names of four things that can use either batteries or mains electricity below.

______________________ ______________________

______________________ ______________________

Dear Helper,

Your child has been learning about electricity at school and looking at things that operate using batteries. In this activity, help them to look first for devices that operate using batteries, and then those that can use either batteries or mains. If necessary, help your child write the names of the objects in the second part of the sheet. You might like to reinforce the dangers of mains electricity as you look around the house.

Name:

Electricity Snakes and Ladders

You will need: dice, a shaker and counters.

- Play 'Electricity Snakes and Ladders' with your helper or a friend.

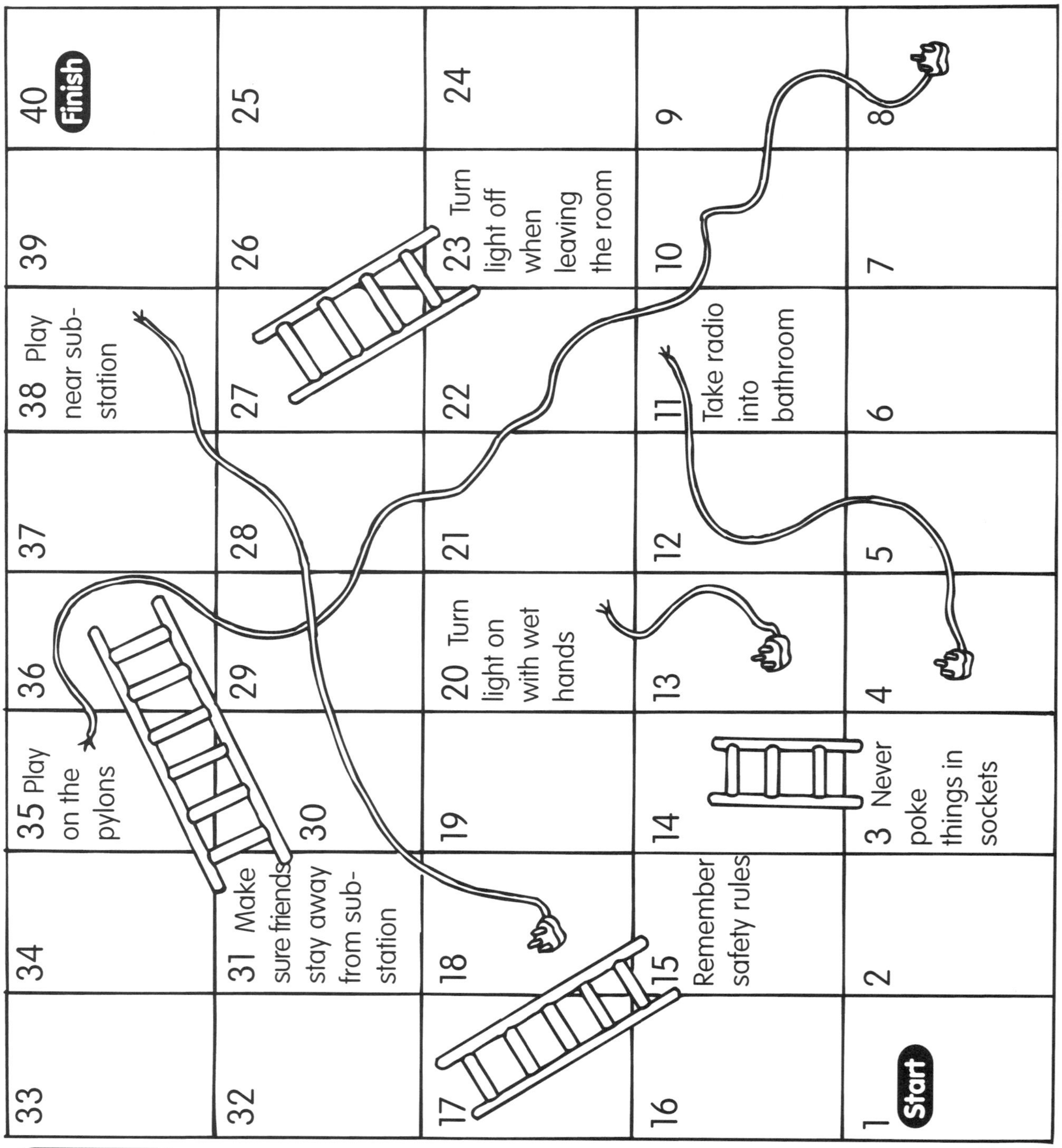

1 Start
2
3 Never poke things in sockets
4
5
6
7
8
9
10
11 Take radio into bathroom
12
13
14
15 Remember safety rules
16
17
18
19
20 Turn light on with wet hands
21
22
23 Turn light off when leaving the room
24
25
26
27
28
29
30
31 Make sure friends stay away from sub-station
32
33
34
35 Play on the pylons
36
37
38 Play near sub-station
39
40 Finish

Dear Helper,

This game should be familiar to your child as they may have played it in class. It's a good game to play as a group, and you will be helping to reinforce some of the things your child has learned about electricity. They will also learn to follow the numbers around the board, how to take turns and that playing games with other people can be enjoyable and fun. As you play, talk with your child about how to keep safe from electricity. You might like to keep this game and play it on a more regular basis.

Name:

Me moving

- Draw a picture of yourself moving in some way.
- Make sure it is different from the one you drew at school.
- Colour it in carefully and cut it out ready to stick on the class display back at school.

Dear Helper,

Your child has been learning about forces by moving in different ways. Moving your body involves forces – you push against the floor to walk, run, skip or hop; you pull with your arms when climbing a rope or climbing frame. Encourage your child to talk about the movements they have made in class, and how they are using a force when they move their bodies. Ask them to select one of their favourite movements from the lesson and to do a detailed drawing of themselves making this movement. Ask: *Are you using a push or a pull?* If you have a long mirror available, they could watch themselves making the movement before drawing their picture.

Name:

Using forces to move things

- When do you use forces every day to move things?
- Think of as many examples as you can.

I use a pull to:

I use a push to:

I use a twist to:

Dear Helper,

Many everyday actions involve a force in the form of a push or a pull (for example, pulling a chair out from the table and pushing it back, pushing food onto a fork or pulling a comb through hair). Help your child to interpret some everyday activities as either a push or a pull and encourage them to fill them in on the sheet. A twist is a combination of a push and a pull (for example, turning a tap on and off). You could try out some of these actions; encourage your child to tell you which force they are using each time. This will help reinforce the work on forces your child has been doing at school.

Name:

Using forces to change a shape

- Look at the pictures of things down the side of the page. Think about which ones you could change the shape of by using a pushing, pulling, squeezing or twisting force.
- Draw them in the space below.

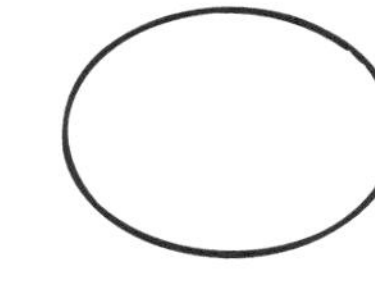

I could use a force to change the shape of these things:

Dear Helper,

This activity will help your child learn that they can use a force to change the shape of some things. Look at each object in turn and talk about whether you could change the shape using a push, pull, squeeze or twist. The objects that could be changed in shape are the play dough, sponge, can, lipstick, toothpaste tube, bulldog clip, egg, cake and teddy bear. Challenge your child to think of some more objects that they could change the shape of.

Name:

Blow football

You will need: two straws and a small ball (a ping-pong ball or a piece of screwed-up paper will do).

- Start with the ball in the centre circle. Blow gently through the straw and try to blow the ball into your opponent's goal.
- Your straw should not touch the ball. When a goal has been scored, put the ball back in the centre circle.
- The winner is the first person to score three goals, or whoever has the highest score after five minutes – you choose!

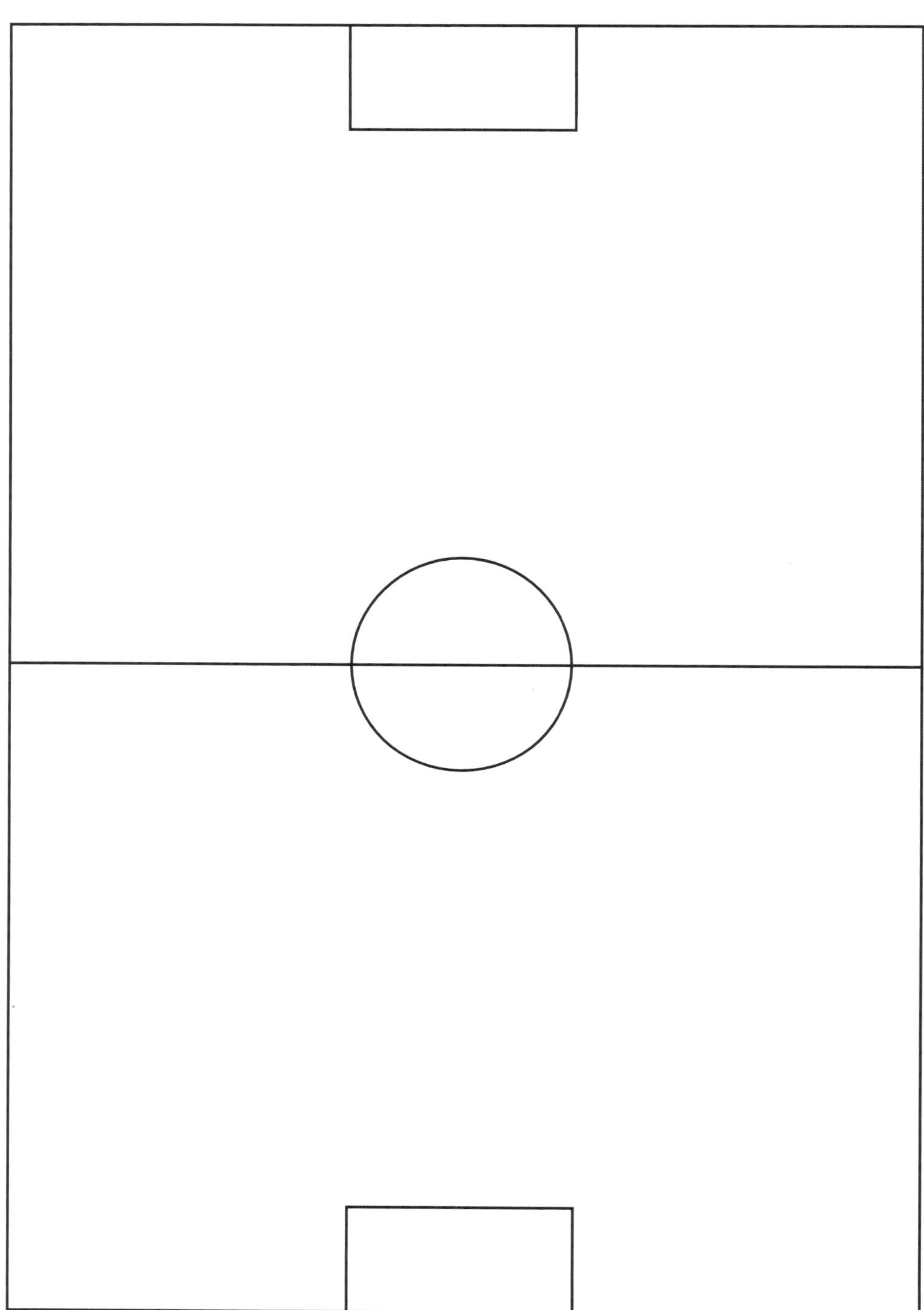

Dear Helper,

This is a fun game to play and will help your child to learn that moving air (wind) is a force. If you wish, you could make a bigger playing surface and involve more people (this might require a referee!). Organise a local league perhaps! As you play, ask your child to explain what is moving the ball (it is being pushed by the air from the straw).

Name:

Pushing down and pushing up

You will need: a collection of unbreakable objects to put in the bath (or in the sink), such as a plastic bottle with a top, a sponge, a ball, a plastic plate, a spoon, a jug, a flannel, a pebble and so on.

- Put your objects into the bath or into a big bowl of water.

Which ones sank to the bottom? ______________________

____

Which floated? ______________________

____

- Now try pushing the ones that float under the water one by one.

Which one was the hardest to push down?

____

How does the water help some things to float?

____

____

Dear Helper,

Your child has been learning that water has an upward force (called *upthrust*) that helps some things to float. This activity will help to reinforce what they have been learning at school and give them the chance to experience the upward 'push' of the water on an object. If you have an empty soft drinks bottle, try pushing the bottle down with the lid on. Fill the bottle with water and try again. A beach ball or plastic football will also demonstrate the upward push. Encourage your child to talk about what is happening as they play, and to describe what they can feel when they push down. If necessary, help them write their sentence to complete the sheet.

Name:

In the dark

- Look around your bedroom with the light on.

- What can you see? Write a list or draw pictures.

With the light on I can see:

- Now switch the light off.
- What can you see now?

With the light off I can only see:

Dear Helper,

It's obviously best to do this activity after dark if possible. Children often think that light comes from their eyes and that this allows them to see; this isn't true, and this activity will help your child learn that we need a source of light in order to see things. The room may not be completely dark even with the light off and the curtains drawn, but talk about how much easier it is to see things when there is light. It might be fun to play 'Blindfold tag' with the whole family: one member of the family is blindfolded, and has to 'catch' and correctly identify another player. Talk about why you cannot see with a blindfold on. (Because the blindfold prevents light from entering our eyes.)

Name:

Light

- Look around your home and make a note of all the light sources you can find.
- Count them and complete this chart.

Type of light source	How many?
ceiling lights	
wall lights	
table lamps	
torches	
candles	
televisions	
fires	

- Did you find any other sources of light?
- Make a list. ______________________________

____

____

- Are there any lights outside? Where are they? What are they used for?

Dear Helper,

Nowadays we have many sources of light – some fixed, some portable, and some we may not think of as sources of light, such as televisions or microwaves. This activity will help your child appreciate the range of light sources in the home, and help develop their writing skills. Encourage your child to look around for as many light sources as possible. Ceiling or table lights are fairly obvious, but help them to realise that the TV gives out light, too, and note any more unusual light sources. Talk about why we have portable light sources such as torches or lanterns. (To help us see where there isn't normally light.)

Name:

Very bright

- Look for the light sources in and around your home.

Which is the brightest?

Which is the dimmest?

- Complete these sentences.

The ______________________ is the brightest.

It needs to be bright because ______________________

____

____

The ______________________ is the dimmest.

This is because ______________________

____

____

- Are there any lights in your home that are just for decoration? What are they and where are they?

____

____

Dear Helper,

We use light in lots of different ways and for different purposes. Help your child think about why we use a certain kind of light for a certain job. Talk about how a bright light helps if we are doing fine work or reading or writing; a dim night light might help us sleep, and we may use soft lights, such as candles, merely for decoration. Your child may need help to write the sentences to complete the sheet. Challenge your child to think of other situations in which we might need different kinds of light.

Name:

In an emergency

In an emergency, which telephone number would you dial? ______________

- Join the picture up to the emergency service you would call.

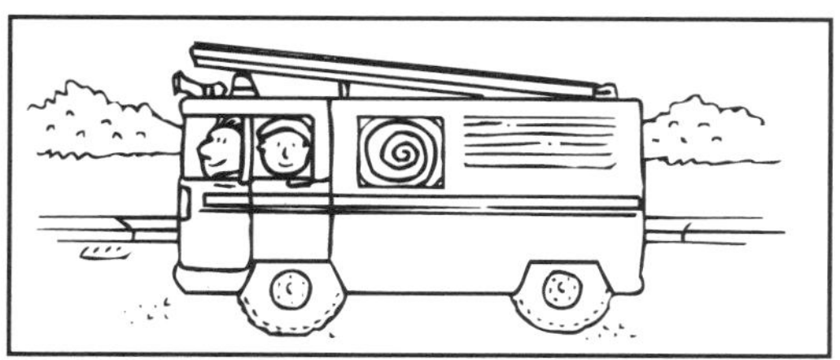

- If you call the emergency services they will need to know your name and address.
- Write it in the box.

Dear Helper,

Your child has been learning what to do in an emergency. You never know when a situation may arise, and it's important that even young children learn their name and address and how to call for help, just in case they need to. It's also useful if they learn their phone number. Stress to your child that they should only dial 999 in a real emergency, because a hoax call may prevent the emergency services from going to someone who really needs help. When completing the sheet, ask your child how they would know which emergency service to ask for in each of the pictures.

Name:

Sounds at home

- When you get home, sit still for a few minutes and listen to all the sounds you can hear.

Can you hear voices?

Are there any animal sounds?

You might hear some machinery or traffic.

- Draw pictures of some of the things that are making sounds.

Dear Helper,

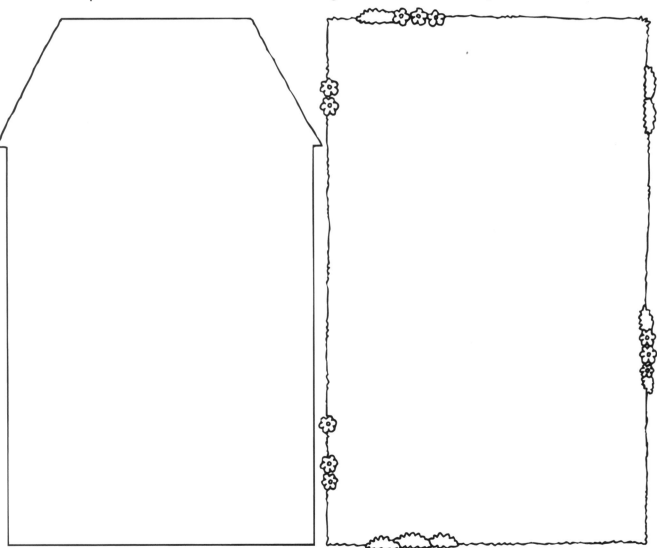

This activity will encourage your child to listen to and identify different sources of sound in the local environment. Listen together for sounds such as footsteps, doors opening or closing, radios or televisions, people talking or dogs barking, traffic and so on. After you have listened, ask your child to think about what is making the sound and where it's coming from. Do they think it is ever completely quiet? Is there always sound around them? Why is this? Can they think of a place where it might be completely quiet?

Name:

UNIT 7 LIGHT & SOUND | SOURCES OF LIGHT AND SOUND

Making music

- Collect some things that you think will make a sound when you tap them with a wooden spoon. You could try to find a pan, a cardboard box and a plastic tub.
- Tap each object gently with a wooden spoon and remember the sound each makes.
- Can you make up a tune to play with your helper?
- Draw a picture of you and your helper surrounded by the instruments you used.

Dear Helper,

This is a potentially noisy activity, so you may wish to warn the neighbours! The noise can be lessened by wrapping a dishcloth around the wooden spoon to muffle the sound. Your child has been looking at things that make sounds in class, and this will help them to experience a variety of objects that can be used to make sounds. Encourage your child to change the volume of the sounds they make by hitting the objects with more or less force; challenge them to put the objects in order of the sound they make. Try using the 'instruments' to accompany a familiar nursery rhyme. If you have a tape recorder, you could record the tune and send it in to school.

PHOTOCOPIABLE

Name:

Nasty noises

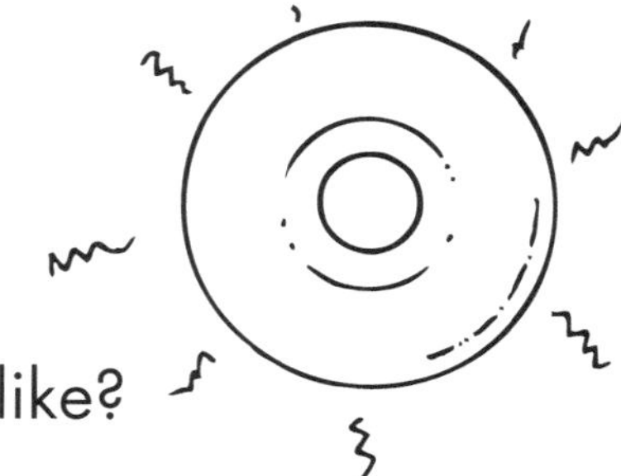

- Some sounds are pleasant to listen to, but others are not so pleasant.
- What are some of the sounds you like and dislike?

I have heard these nice sounds: ______________________

____

The most pleasant sound I heard was ______________________

____

____

These are the sounds I didn't like: ______________________

____

____

The most unpleasant noise I heard was ______________________

____

____

Dear Helper,

These days, children often seem to simply ignore sounds around them. This activity will encourage them to listen to and discriminate between the sounds they hear. They should begin to think about the sounds they like and find pleasant to listen to, and those that they find unpleasant. Talk about why they like or dislike particular sounds as they complete the sentences on the sheet. Do they think that everyone finds the same noises unpleasant? Remind them that very loud sounds could damage their hearing.

Name:

Helpful sounds

- Some sounds warn us that something is happening, or that there is a danger of some kind.

How many helpful sounds did you hear this week?

On Monday I heard	
On Tuesday I heard	
On Wednesday I heard	
On Thursday I heard	
On Friday I heard	
On Saturday I heard	
On Sunday I heard	

Dear Helper,

Some 'helpful' sounds give us information, for example the ping of the microwave tells us that food is cooked. Others, such as the peep of a lorry reversing, warn of possible danger. Police and other emergency vehicles use sirens to warn of their approach so we can clear their way. As you complete this sound diary, point out warning sounds to help your child to understand how their hearing helps keep them safe.

Name:

Moon watch

- The Moon appears to change shape.
- Sometimes you can see the Moon in the sky before you go to bed, and sometimes you can see it in the morning on your way to school.
- Keep a diary. Draw the shape of the Moon every three days or so.
- If you can't see because there is too much cloud, try the next day.

Date	Time	Shape of Moon

Date	Time	Shape of Moon

- Colour in the shape that the Moon really is.

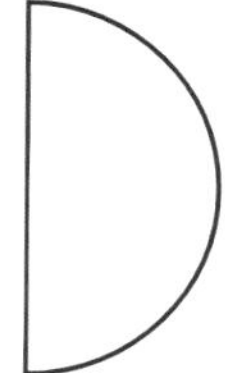
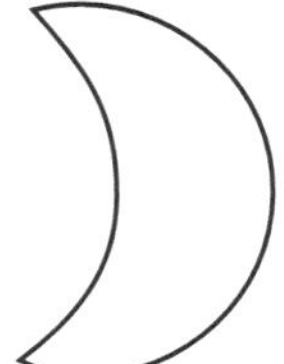
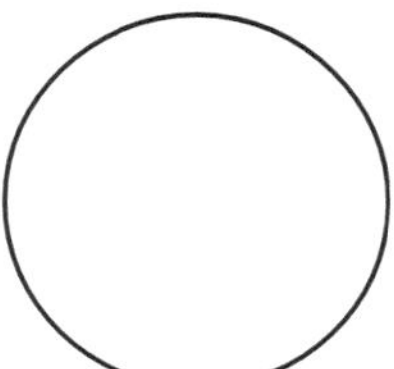

Dear Helper,

Your child has been learning about the Moon in class. Keeping a diary over the course of a month will develop your child's skills of observation and their understanding of the fact that the Moon appears to change shape as it goes through its monthly cycle. The Moon is a sphere that does not really change shape, but the way it reflects the Sun's light makes it appear to do so. This is difficult for young children to understand, so talk to them about it as much as possible. You might like to share in this task, making the observations part of your daily routine, and helping to draw the Moon shapes on the sheet. Your child's teacher will have told them whether to start the diary in the morning or the evening. A full Moon is only seen in the middle hours of the night, so your child may not see this.

Name:

Sun, Moon and stars

You will need: scissors and glue.

Sun **Moon** **Earth**

Our Sun is a ______________________. We see most stars as

tiny dots of light because ______________________________

____

The Sun is our nearest ________________.

- Look at the pictures above. Which one is a star? Cut out the star here and stick it over the correct picture.

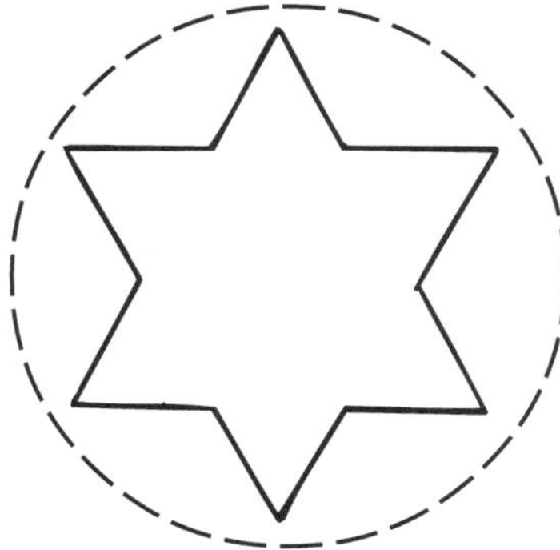

Dear Helper,

The Sun is a star. It is our nearest star, which is why it appears so much larger in the sky than the other stars that are much further away. This activity will help your child to understand the difference between the Sun (a star), the Earth (a planet) and the Moon (a satellite of the Earth). Help your child to complete the sentences, then to decide which of the pictures is really a star, sticking the star shape over it. Make sure that they know never to look directly at the Sun, as it is very dangerous and could damage their eyes.

Name:

Night work

- Some people have to work at night.
- Do you know anybody who does?
- Ask your helper if they know somebody who works at night.
- Draw pictures of them at work in the spaces, and write what they do underneath.

Dear Helper,

It's important for your child to know how the pattern of day and night affects people. If you know anyone who works at night, it may help your child to think of them and what they do as they complete this sheet. Talk about other jobs that people may do at night to fill in the rest of the spaces on the sheet. People who work for the emergency services are fairly obvious, but encourage your child to think of people who work stacking shelves in supermarkets, in 24-hour petrol stations, or journalists and printers who are getting tomorrow's newspapers ready. Discuss why some people have to work at night and why their jobs are important to all of us.

Name:

Food groups

- Draw some pictures of foods that fit into each of these food groups.

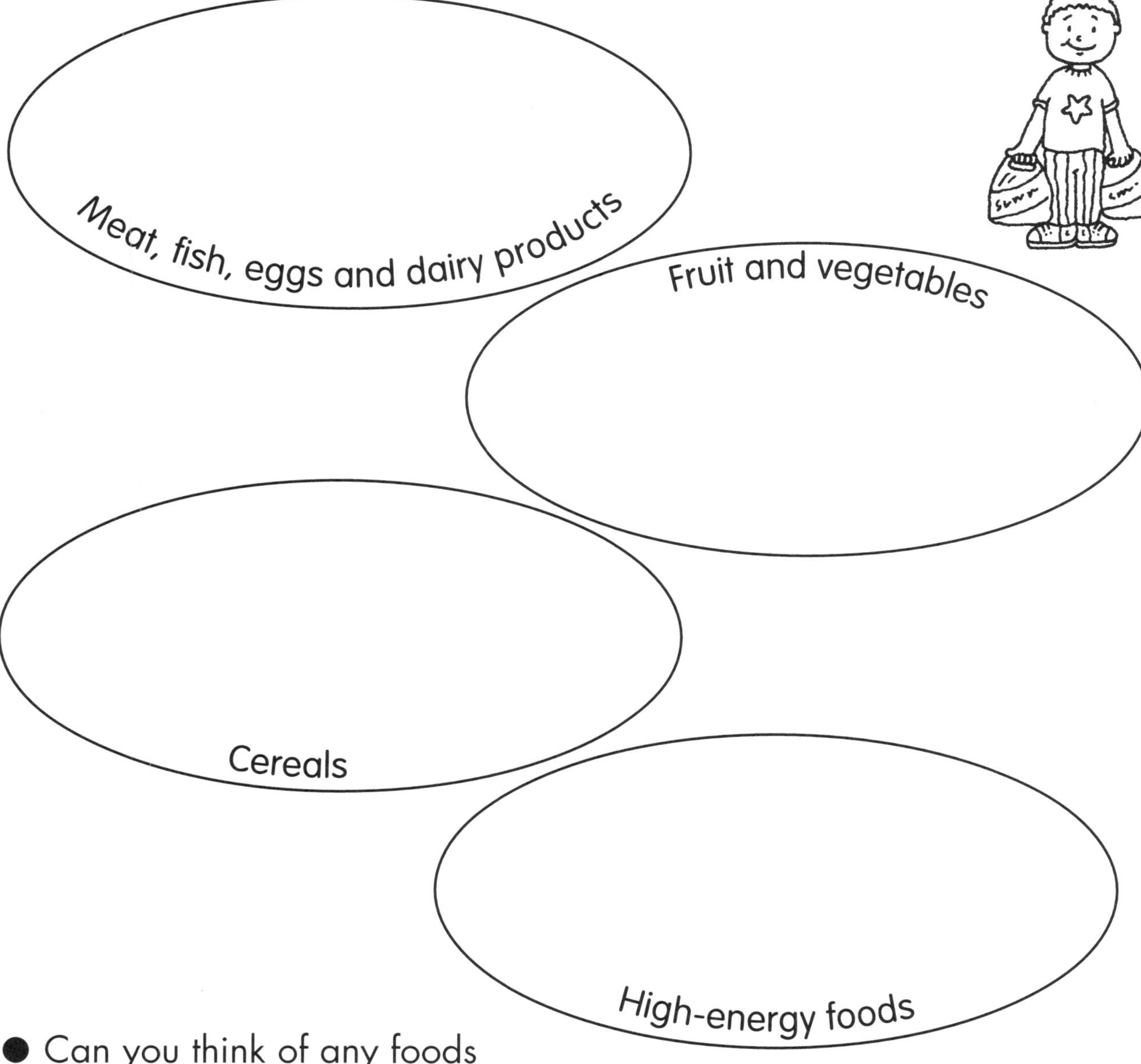

- Can you think of any foods that could be put into more than one food group? Write their names here.

Dear Helper,

Your child is learning how a knowledge of food groups can help us to eat a healthy, balanced diet. When preparing food with your child, talk about which of the four groups above each food belongs to; help them to identify two or three foods for each group. Challenge them to name some foods that might fall into more than one category, such as cheese on toast (dairy and cereal) or fruit yoghurt (dairy and fruit).

Name:

Exercise diary

● Keep a record of the exercise you do in one week.

Day	At school	At home
Monday		
Tuesday		
Wednesday		
Thursday		
Friday		
Saturday		
Sunday		

● Colour in any of the exercises that you do regularly.

My favourite sort of exercise is

____

Dear Helper,

Regular exercise is an important part of keeping healthy. This diary will help your child identify any regular exercise they do. Ask them to tell you about exercise they have done at school today, including any aspects of PE (and even vigorous play), then encourage them to record this in the diary, helping with writing if necessary. Add any exercise they have done at home to complete the day's entry – don't forget everyday activities like walking to school. They should repeat this each day until the diary is full, then bring it back to school.

Name:

Sleep diary

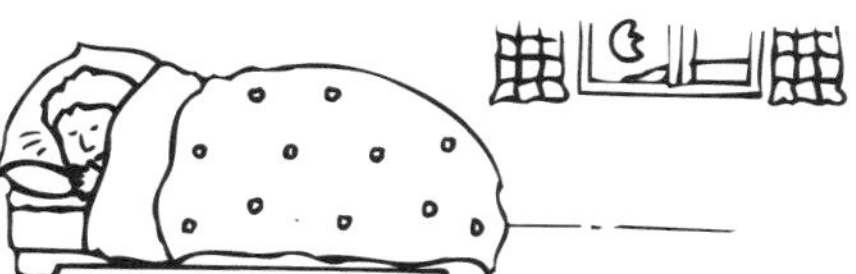

- Keep a sleep diary for a week.

Day	I went to bed at	I got up at	I slept for (hours)
Monday			
Tuesday			
Wednesday			
Thursday			
Friday			
Saturday			
Sunday			

How many hours did you sleep during the whole week?

On which night did you sleep for the longest time? ____________________

On which night did you sleep for the shortest time? ____________________

Dear Helper,

At this age, your child needs to understand that sufficient sleep is one of the things that helps to keep them healthy. Talk about how sleep gives our bodies and our brains rest to help them grow and develop, and that too little sleep makes us tired, grumpy and makes it difficult to concentrate. It would be good if you could make filling in the sleep diary part of the bedtime routine. You may need to help your child to tell the time and write it down in the diary, and to work out the number of hours they have slept for. The questions about the number of hours slept are quite difficult, and your child may need help to answer them.

Name:

Cleaning teeth

- Draw a picture of your toothbrush and toothpaste.
- Put in as much detail as you can.
- Look at the information on a toothpaste tube to see what the toothpaste is made from.

- Is there any fluoride in your toothpaste?
- Tick the boxes to show when you clean your teeth.

Day	Morning	Evening
Monday		
Tuesday		
Wednesday		
Thursday		
Friday		
Saturday		
Sunday		

Dear Helper,

Cleaning teeth regularly (ideally twice a day) is an important aspect of personal hygiene and helps to keep teeth and gums healthy. Encourage your child to clean their teeth properly by making sure they understand how important it is to clean the back and front of all their teeth with an up-and-down motion. Most toothpastes now contain fluoride, which helps make teeth stronger and resist decay. Remind your child to fill in their diary after they clean their teeth.

Name:

Bath time

- After you have had a bath or shower, talk to your helper about how you get yourself clean.
- Tell them why it is important to keep clean.
- Draw a picture of yourself having a bath or a shower.

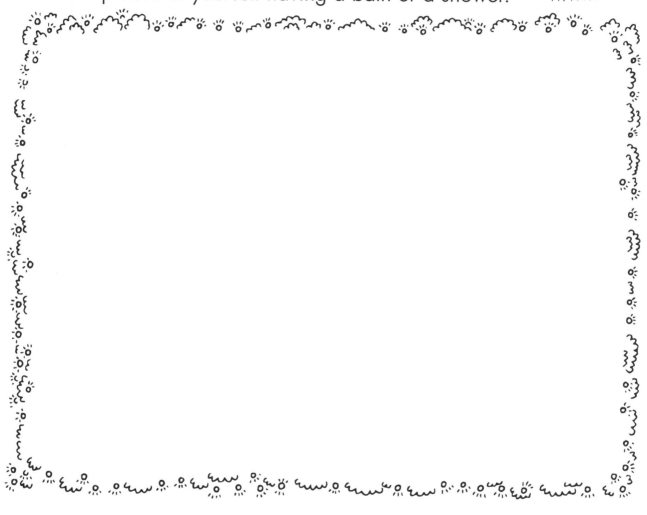

- Put all the things you use to keep yourself clean into the picture.
- Make a list of them on the bathroom shelf.

Dear Helper,

This activity will help your child understand the importance of keeping themselves clean. Talk to them about the fact that many illnesses, particularly tummy upsets, can be caused by eating or handling food with dirty hands, and that our bodies would get smelly and sore if we did not keep ourselves clean.

Name:

People who care

- This is how people cared for me this week.

Who?	What?	When?
Dad	*Ironed my shirt*	*Saturday*

Dear Helper,

As they are growing up, young children need a lot of care from adults. This activity will help your child appreciate the things that others do for them. As they fill in the sheet, talk to them about how they are being helped. Include things like reading bedtime stories, which help children develop their language and imagination, as well as the more practical things like washing and preparing meals. Help your child realise that things like ironing, shopping, and cleaning their bedroom are all aspects of caring that may (or may not!) be done for them.

Name:

How we change

- Ask an older person how their appearance has changed as they have grown older.
- For example, they might now need to wear spectacles.
- Make notes about three or four important changes in the space below, then draw a picture of them as they are now.

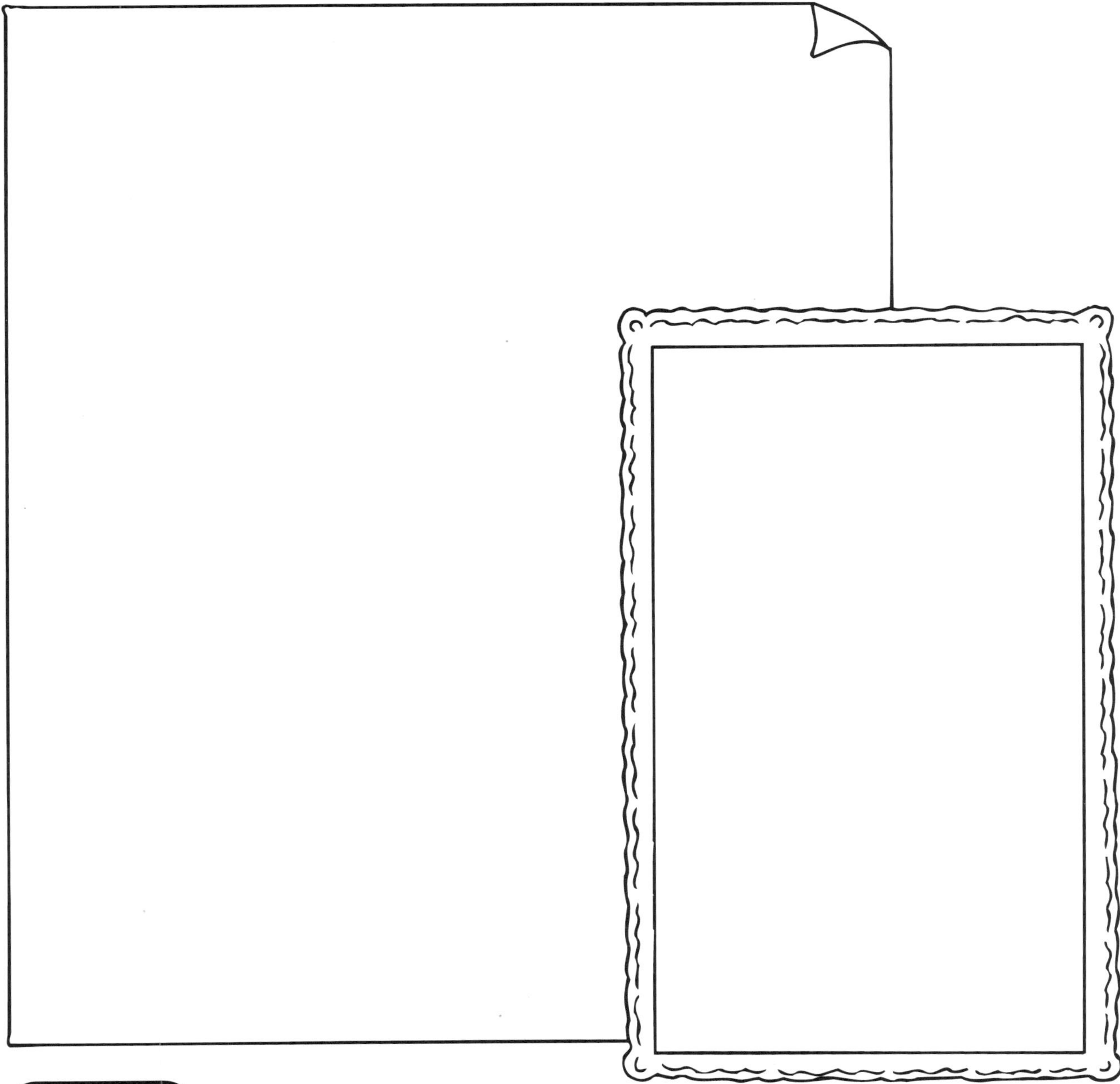

Dear Helper,

Your child has been looking at how our appearance changes as we get older. Because this happens so slowly, they may not notice it happening; this activity will help develop the idea. Encourage them to talk to an older person (a grandparent would be ideal), so that they can note some obvious changes. After they have talked and made notes (you might like to help them with this), encourage them to put as much detail into their drawings as possible.

Name:

Plant or animal?

- Look at each row of pictures.
- Put a cross through the odd one out and colour in the others.

Dear Helper,

Your child is learning to tell the difference between plants and animals. As they complete each line, ask them to tell you how they know which is the odd one out. Talk about the similarities and differences between plants and animals (animals can move and need to eat food; both plants and animals grow and need water).

Name:

UNIT 2 ANIMALS & PLANTS | GROWING UP

Animal or plant?

- Colour in the picture.
- Write **P** for plant by all the plants you can see.
- Write **A** for animal by all the animals.

How many plants did you find? | |

How many animals did you find? | |

Dear Helper,

Look at the picture with your child and help them decide which things are plants and which animals. Ask them to tell you how they decided which category some of the things belong to, as some children find it difficult to appreciate that birds and insects are both part of the animal kingdom.

PHOTOCOPIABLE

Name:

My plant

- Look in a book to find out about a plant.
- Choose an unusual one if you like.
- Draw your plant and ask your helper to help you write down some of the things you found out about it.

My plant is called ______________________________

It looks like this:

I found out these things about it: ______________________________

____

____

____

Dear Helper,

Your child is learning to use books and other sources of information for research. If possible, go to the library and look for books on plants, together choosing a suitable book. Help them to note and adapt important things from the text, not just to copy it. Look for things such as height, colour, country of origin, the type of soil the plant likes, and so on. They may need help with the writing, but encourage them to work independently if possible. If you can't visit the library, books or magazines at home, or the Internet are equally useful sources.

Name:

At the supermarket

- Go to the local shop with your helper.
- Look at the fruits, seeds, nuts and pulses that you can see.
- Write some of them in the spaces below.

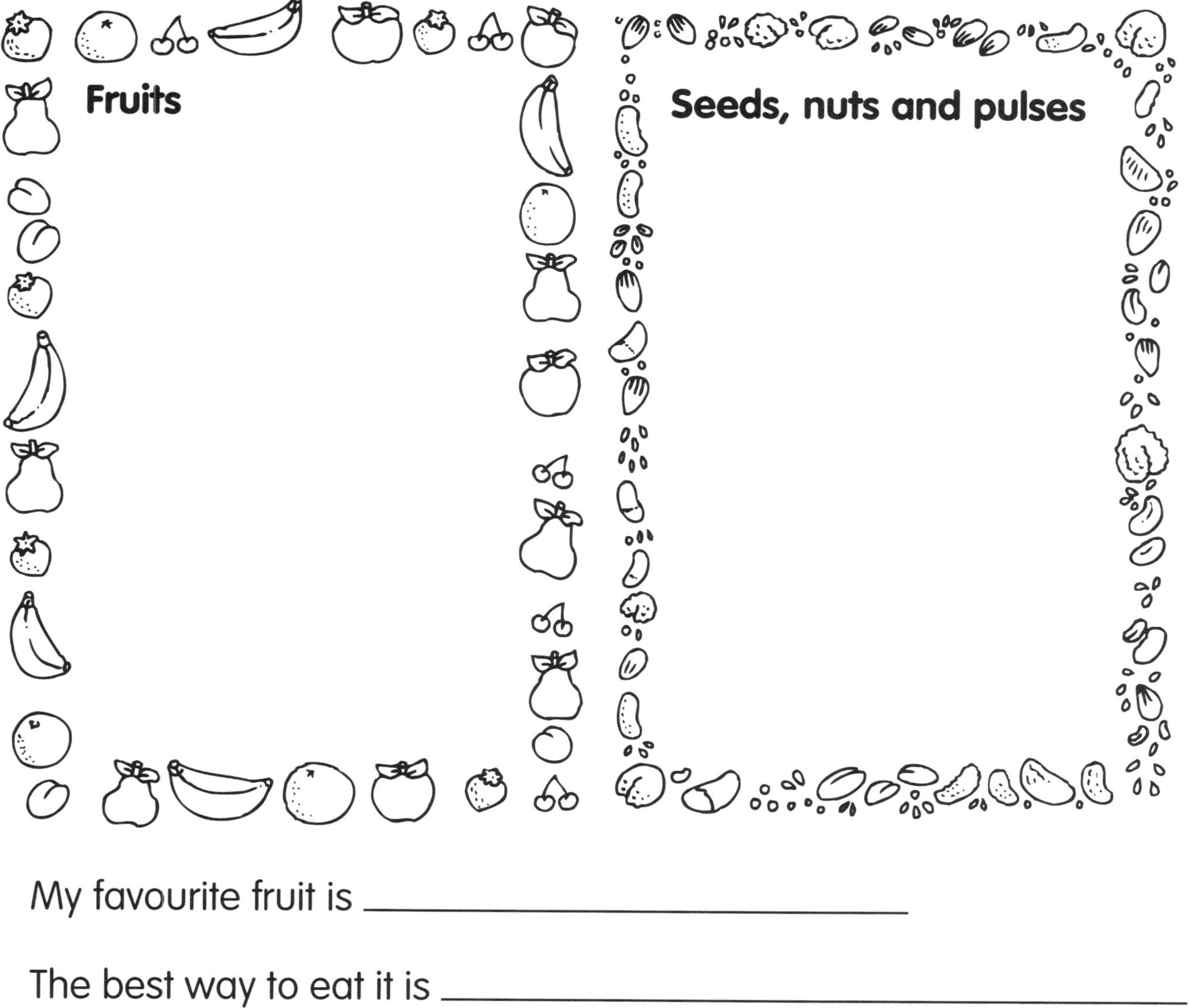

My favourite fruit is ______________________________

The best way to eat it is ____

____

____

Dear Helper,

This activity will help your child learn about the variety of fruits, seeds, nuts and pulses that we eat. Take your child to the local shop, market or supermarket and look at the variety that is available. Talk about those that they are familiar with and discuss how you might use them. Look for any unusual examples and think about how you might use those. Encourage your child to think about their favourite fruit and to write down the best way of eating it, or a recipe for cooking it.

Name:

Seedy?

- Look carefully at all the things you eat this week.
- Which things have seeds in?
- Draw pictures and label them.

All these things had seeds in: ______________________

____

____

We ate the seeds in these things: ______________________

____

We threw these seeds away: ______________________

____

Which food had the most seeds? ______________________

- Try planting one or two of the seeds you have found and see if they grow.

Dear Helper,

Many of the foods we eat have seeds in them. Encourage your child to help you prepare any fruits or vegetables you are going to eat and look for seeds as you do so. To help develop counting skills, challenge them to count the seeds they can find in some of the fruit or vegetables – you may be able to count the seeds (pips) in apples, grapes or oranges, but tomatoes, cucumbers or bananas may contain too many to count. If you decide to plant some seeds, orange, lemon or grapefruit seeds usually grow well if cared for.

Name:

Animal groups

You will need: scissors and glue.

- Cut out the pictures and stick them into the right group.

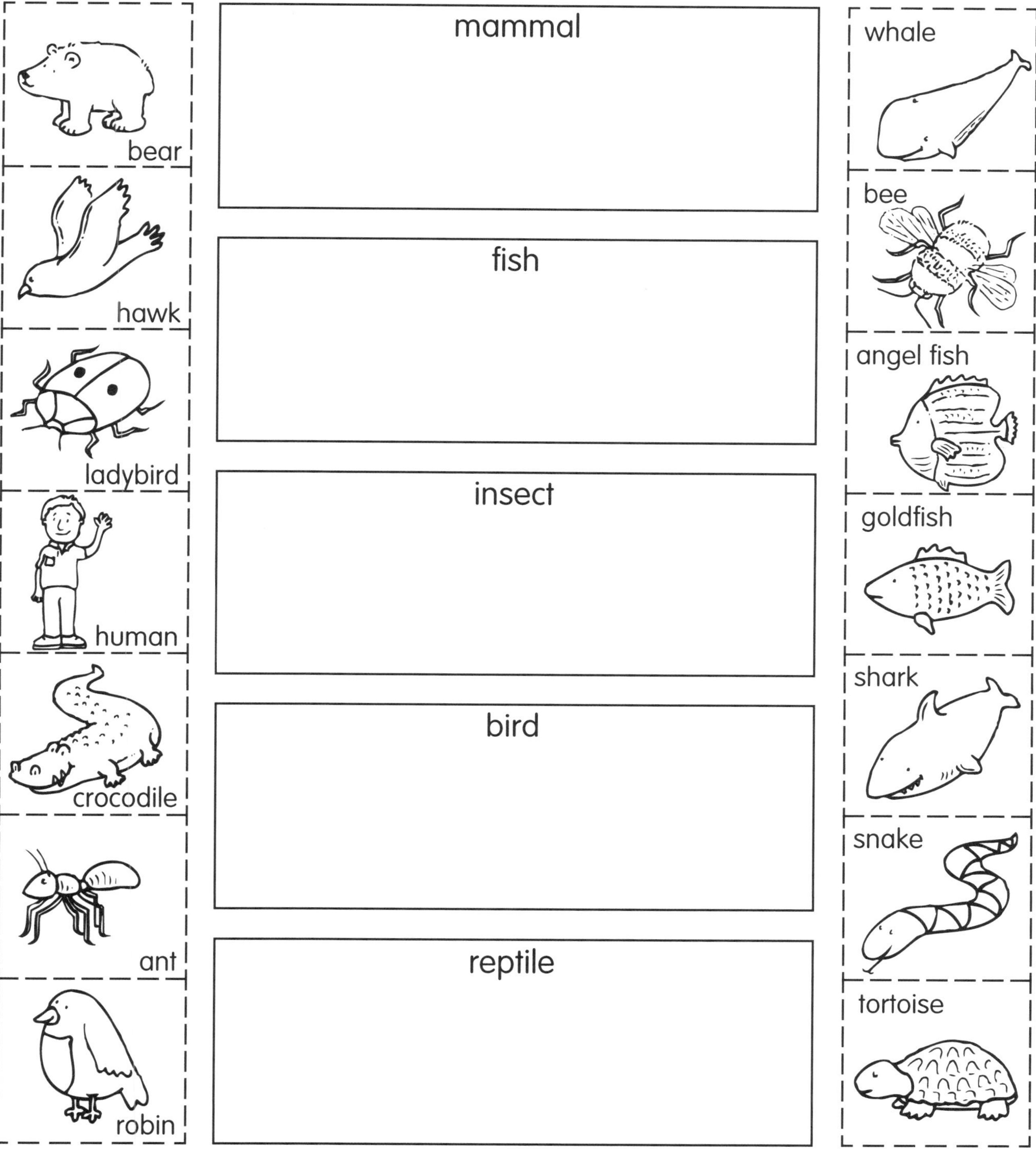

Dear Helper,

Your child has been learning about animals belonging to different groups. Sorting these pictures will help to reinforce this idea. Encourage them to place the pictures into the correct groups before sticking them onto the sheet, and talk about why they have decided to put an animal into a particular group. Remind your child, if necessary, that whales are mammals, and need to breathe air just like human beings.

Name:

Native animals

- Use reference books or the Internet to find out about an unusual animal that comes from this country.
- Draw your animal and write about it with your helper.

My animal is ______________________________

My animal is

____

____

____

Dear Helper,

Finding out about things from books and other sources is an important skill that this activity will help to develop. Choose an animal, read all about it together and encourage your child to note important facts rather than just copying out sections of text. (This is particularly important if you have access to the Internet where information can easily be copied and pasted.) You may need to help your child with the writing about their animal, but encourage them to use their own words. If you can, visit a pet shop or a wildlife park to find out more about your chosen animal.

Name:

Butterfly changes

You will need: scissors and glue.

- Cut out the pictures and stick them in the spaces in the correct order to show how a butterfly grows and changes.

- Can you name each of the stages?
- Write the names of the stages underneath the pictures.

Dear Helper,

Your child has been learning that animals reproduce and change as they get older. This activity will show them that some animals go through more noticeable changes than others. If you have access to a park or garden, you might like to go out and look for caterpillars, butterflies and moths – sometimes you can find chrysalises (pupae) in sheltered places. Remind your child to always treat living things with respect. Talk about butterflies laying eggs, which then hatch into caterpillars. The caterpillar grows and, when it is big enough, turns into a chrysalis, from which a butterfly emerges.

Name:

I-spy plants and animals

- See how many of the plants and animals on this list you can spot this week. Write down on which day you first saw them.

Name	Day
dandelion	
oak tree	
horse chestnut tree	
elderberry	
Buddleia	
willow herb	
daisy	
ant	
snail	
wasp	
worm	
dog	
pigeon	
sparrow	
ladybird	
bee	
fly	

- Do you see any other plants or animals? Write their names on the back of this sheet.

Dear Helper,

This activity will help your child learn the names of some plants and animals in the local environment. Keep a look out on the way to and from school, in the garden, or take your child on a plant- and animal-spotting walk. Challenge your child to identify the names of less familiar plants and animals using books from home or the library.

Name:

Comparing plants

- Go into the garden or local park and choose two plants to look at.
- Draw a leaf from each plant.

How are they similar? ______

How are they different? ______

- Draw a flower from each plant.

How are they similar? ______

How are they different? ______

- Look at a fruit or seed head from each plant.

How are they similar? ______

How are they different? ______

Dear Helper,

By looking carefully at two different plants your child will learn to notice the similarities and differences between them. Encourage them to draw and describe the things they observe in as much detail as possible. (For example, look at the shape and colour of the leaves and petals, or whether there are prickles on the stems. Are the flowers scented? Do they grow to different heights?) You might like to make notes of your child's observations for them. If you have a magnifying glass, use it to see even more. If there's no garden or park nearby, a garden centre or flowers from the supermarket will do.

Name:

Seashore

- How many plants and animals can you think of whose habitat is the seashore?
- Draw and label some of the things you can think of on this picture.
- You could use reference books or the Internet to help you.

Dear Helper,

The seashore may be relatively unfamiliar to your child, but this activity will help them to learn about the variety of plants and animals in a less familiar habitat. If you have been to the seaside, talk with your child about what they remember seeing there. It might be useful to visit the library for some simple reference books to help with research.

Name:

Who needs what?

- Next to each picture, write down some things that the animal needs in its habitat.
- Underline the living things that they depend on. The first one is done for you as an example.
- Choose from the words in the box to help you. You might want to use some words more than once. Can you think of any other creatures that the animals might depend on?

thrush	seeds trees snails water
frog	
hedgehog	
bee	
woodlouse	

slugs	**pollen**	**insects**	**nectar**	**trees**	**flowers**
worms	**rotting vegetation**		**water**	**pond**	**damp**
dark	**hedge**	**bushes**	**snails**	**seeds**	**leaf litter**

Dear Helper,

Living things in a habitat depend on each other for food and shelter, and non-living things such as ponds or leaf litter are also important. Completing this activity will help your child understand this dependence. Look at the list of words with your child, help them to write the correct words against each animal and underline the living things that each depends on. Talk about water – your child may want to add this to every box (this is correct, since all living things need water).

Name:

Seasonal change

You will need: scissors and glue.

- Draw pictures in the spaces below that show how a tree changes in each season.

spring	summer	autumn	winter

- Colour the pictures below. Cut them out and stick them onto another sheet of paper in two rows that show the order of the seasons: spring, summer, autumn and winter.

Dear Helper,

Putting these pictures in order will help your child learn about the progression of the seasons. Talk to them about the changes that they might see through the year. Play a guessing game before sticking the pictures down by showing your child a picture at a time and asking them to name the season. Alternatively, lay out all the pictures and ask them to choose a picture for the season you say. Challenge your child to match the two pictures for each season.

Name:

In my street

- Survey your street.
- Tick the boxes to show what you find.

What you see	A lot	A little	None
Graffiti			
Trees			
Litter			
Potholes			
Broken windows			
Flowers			
Dog mess			
Broken paving slabs			
Grassy verges			
Parked cars			

- Write down some ideas about how you could improve your environment.

Dear Helper,

It's important that your child learns to care for their immediate surroundings. In order to do this they need to notice both the pleasant and unpleasant aspects of the neighbourhood. Go for a walk together and help your child to make judgements about where to put the ticks on the sheet. Talk with them about any changes they think could be made to improve the environment (you might need to help them to put these thoughts into words on the sheet). Challenge your child to prioritise their list.

Name:

Look for labels

- Look at the labels in some of your clothes to see what they are made from.
- Draw the clothes and write what they are made from underneath.

My ______________ is made from ____________________	My ______________ is made from ____________________

What is the most common type of fabric used to make your clothes?

____

Which of your clothes are made from one type of material only?

____

____

Dear Helper,

This activity will help your child realise that most fabrics these days are made from more than one type of material. Together, find and read the labels in some items of clothing and fill in the spaces above. Remind your child that the word *material* does not just mean fabric when used scientifically. Challenge your child to find fabrics that look very different but are made from the same material (for example, polyester appears in many forms and wool may be a finely woven fabric or a heavy knit).

Name:

Useful materials

- Look around at home.
- See how many things you can find that are made from these materials.

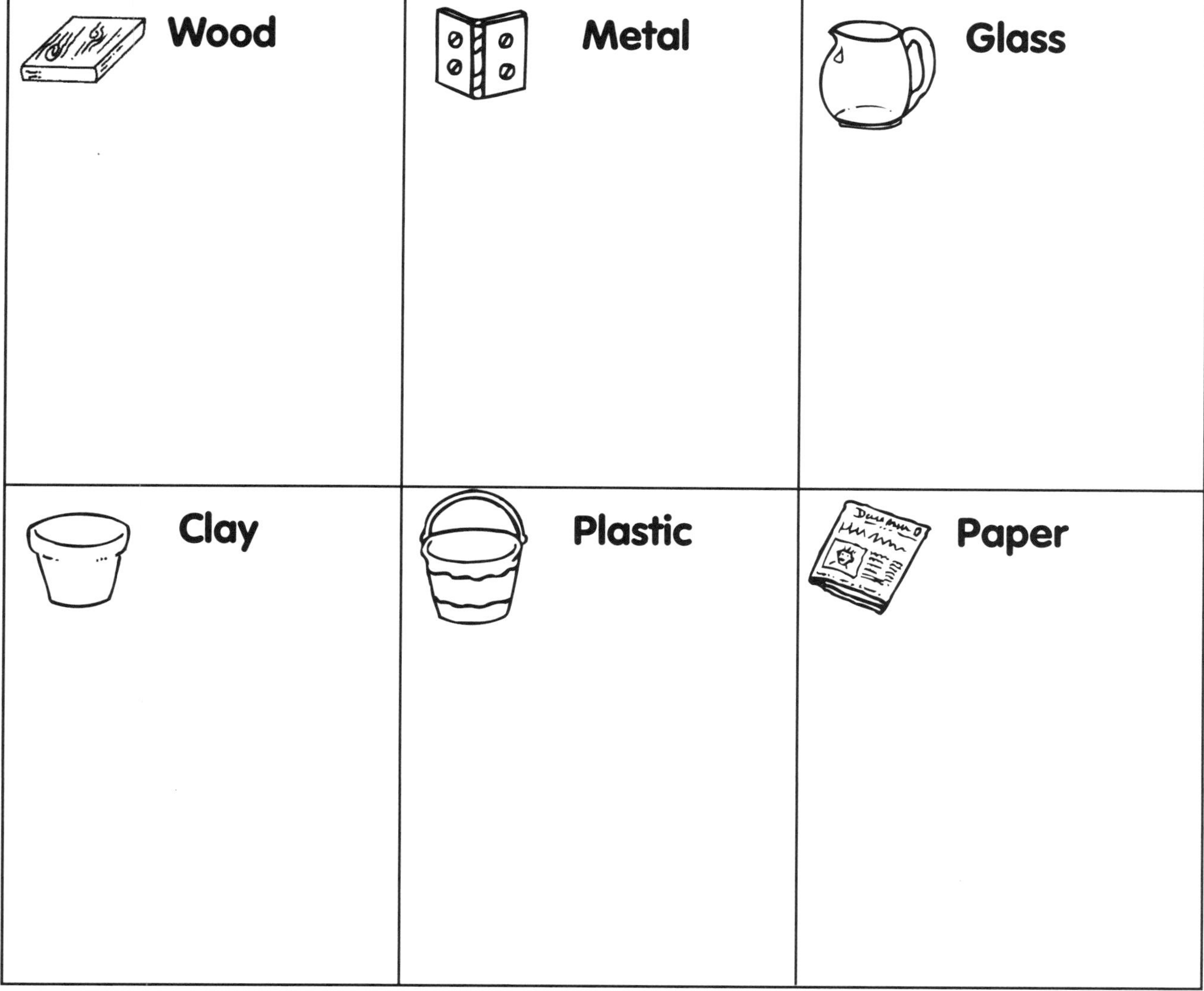

- Choose one of the objects you found and write a few words about why you think it is made from that material.

The ____________________ is made from ______________________

because ____

Dear Helper,

Doing this activity will help your child learn that we use materials every day in a variety of ways. Help them to look around the house and find and list as many objects as possible made from each material. Talk about why a particular object is made from a certain material (for example, a knife is normally made from metal because it is hard, rigid and can be shaped and sharpened).

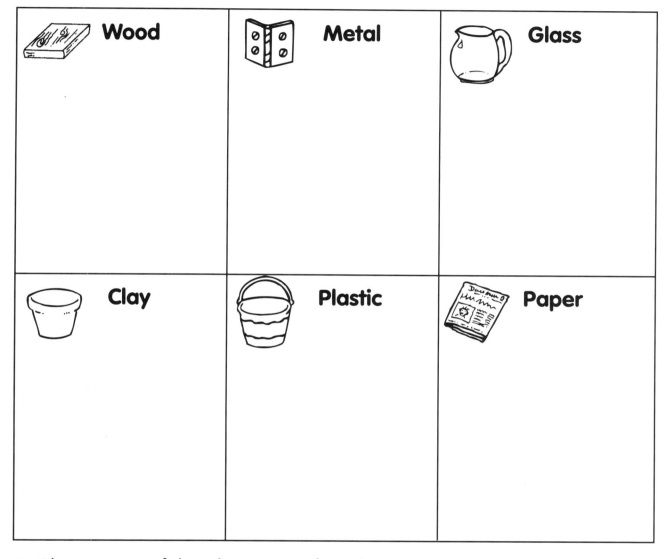

Name:

Natural materials

- What things can you find at home that are made from natural materials such as wood, wool, cotton, leather or stone?
- Draw pictures and label them in the space below.

- Choose two of the natural materials you found and try to find out and write about where they come from.

Dear Helper,

Your child is learning that some materials (such as wool, stone or leather) occur naturally. Help them to identify any such materials in the home and to draw pictures in the space above. It doesn't matter if you can't find examples of all the materials listed. You may have to look closely at labels, as these days it's often hard to distinguish between natural and manufactured materials. Help your child to find out about the origins of two of the materials you found (for example, wool is made from the fleece of sheep). Talk about this, then help your child to write down their ideas.

Name:

It's not natural

Many years ago, people could only use natural materials to build their houses. These days we have many manufactured materials to choose from.

- How many manufactured materials can you find that have been used to build your house?
- Draw them and label them.

Dear Helper,

This activity will help your child learn that some materials are manufactured rather than occurring naturally. Together, look for some of the manufactured materials that have been used to build your home (for example, plastic pipes, metal door handles, concrete floors, glass windows and so on). Talk about how they think these materials have been manufactured, and why they are more suitable for their job than natural materials.

Potato nests

You will need: 700g (1½lb) potatoes, peeled and cut into pieces, salt, 50g (2oz) butter or margarine, a little milk.

⚠ You will need an adult to help with this recipe. Never use the cooker without your helper!

Make potato nests for tea and fill them with whatever you like. Here's what you need to do:

1. Boil the potatoes in salted water for 15–20 minutes until tender, and drain them.

2. Mash the potatoes, using a potato masher or a fork.

3. Mix in the butter and milk, and allow the mixture to cool.

4. Use a fork to divide the mixture into four nest shapes on warm plates, and fill them with the filling of your choice. Serve immediately.

For the fillings, you could use anything you like. Try baked beans, scrambled egg, tuna or diced vegetables.

- Write your recipe for a filling here:

Dear Helper,

Please make sure your child is not left alone with hot pans and ovens, and that you drain the boiling water from the potatoes. Talk about kitchen safety and hygiene rules when handling food. As you make this recipe, talk about how the potatoes change when they are heated (cooked) – this will help your child learn that materials often change when they are heated.

Name:

Look for steam

- Look around your home. Where do you find steam?
- Draw pictures of things that steam below.

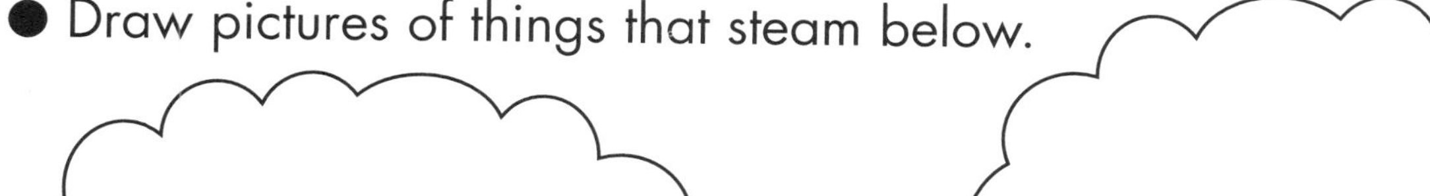

- What happens to steam when it cools?

Dear Helper,

Hot water and steam can be very dangerous, so please make sure that when your child is looking for steam from a boiling kettle or saucepan that you are with them and they keep a safe distance. Talk about how water turns to steam when it is heated, and that when it cools down again it changes back to water (windows are a good place to see this). Encourage your child to think of places other than the kitchen where they may find steam (for example, the bathroom). Think about different times you might see steam: on a cold morning you may be able to see your breath; on a hot day, after rain, you may see roofs or pavements steaming.

Cool it!

Make sure you wash your hands before you begin. You will need an adult to help you.

You will need: a packet of lemon meringue mix and a sponge or pastry case.

- Follow the instructions on the packet to make your lemon meringue pie.
- Describe what you had to do.

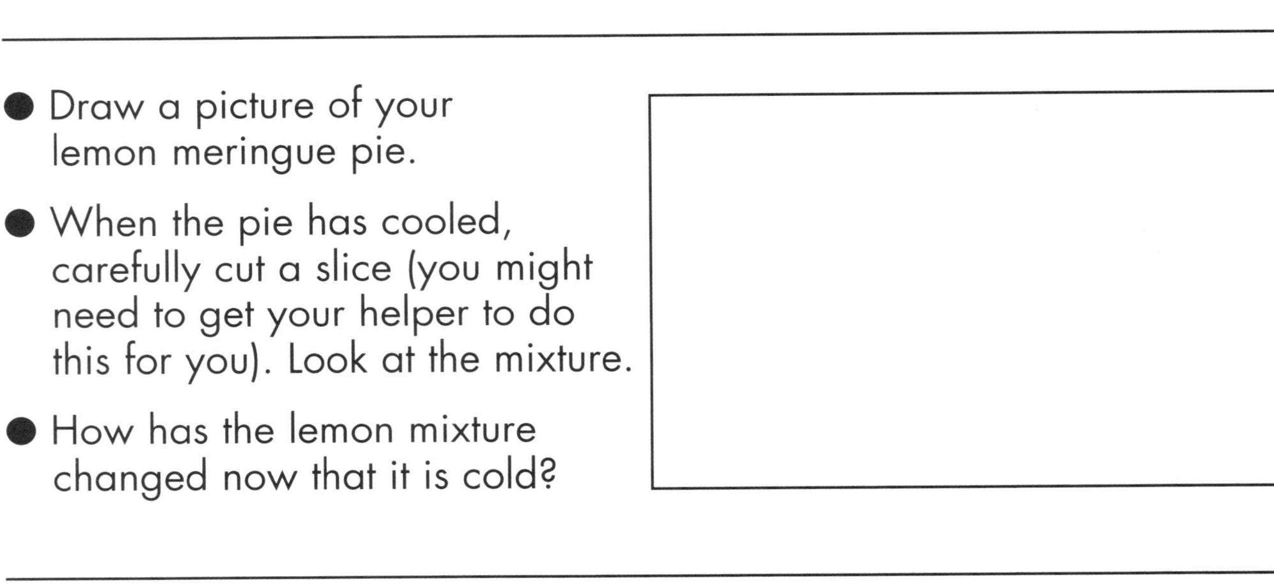

- Draw a picture of your lemon meringue pie.
- When the pie has cooled, carefully cut a slice (you might need to get your helper to do this for you). Look at the mixture.
- How has the lemon mixture changed now that it is cold?

Dear Helper,

Your child is learning that things change when they are cooled. Help them to read and follow the instructions on the packet (make sure they are not left alone with the hot liquid). Look closely at the mixture when it is hot, and notice how runny it is. Look again when it is cold (you might wish to put it in the fridge to make sure it is really cold) and notice how the filling has become solid. Talk about the difference between the hot and cold lemon mixture and describe how it has changed.

Name:

Cheese on toast

You will need: cheese, bread, butter or margarine (optional).

- Try making cheese on toast for tea with your helper. You could add sliced tomatoes, chopped pickled onions, Worcestershire sauce or anything else you like to make it more interesting.
- As you are making your cheese on toast, draw pictures on the back of this sheet that show the following:

the bread before it was toasted
how the bread has changed after toasting
the cheese on the toast before grilling
the cheese after grilling

Never use the toaster or grill without your helper!

1. Toast your bread (you could use the toaster for this).

2. Spread some butter or margarine on it if you wish.

3. Ask your helper to slice or grate some cheese and cover one side of each slice with the cheese.

4. Put the toast under a medium grill until bubbly and golden brown.

5. Enjoy your tea!

Did you try more than one topping on your cheese on toast?

____

Which was your favourite? ________________________

Dear Helper,

Please make sure that you are with your child, and help them to use the toaster or grill safely for this activity. This is also a good opportunity to reinforce rules about hygiene. Making cheese on toast will help your child understand that heating and cooking changes both the cheese and the toast. Talk about how, once toasted, you cannot get the original bread back again; look closely at the melted cheese and talk about how the hot grill has changed it by melting.

Name:

Hot spots

- Look around your house. How many sources of heat can you find?
- Make a list and draw them.

Name and picture of heat source	**What supplies the heat energy? (gas, electricity, oil, solid fuel)**

Dear Helper,

Your child is learning how we get heat energy from a variety of sources, and this activity will show them the variety of different heat sources in the home. Talk about how heat is a form of energy, and help your child to identify sources of heat (for example, an iron that uses electricity to smooth our clothes, or a cooker that uses gas to supply the heat energy that cooks our food). See how many different sources you can find.

Name:

How many ways?

- Look around your house with your helper.
- How many ways of using electricity can you find?
- Make a list.

Name of device	What the electricity does	How we use the device

Dear Helper,

Your child is learning about how we use electricity. Help them to look around the house for as many electrical appliances as you can find, and fill in the boxes on the sheet with them. This will help develop their observation and writing skills. For example, an iron is heated by electricity, and we use it to smooth our clothes. Whenever you talk about electricity, it is a good idea to talk about safety with your child.

Name:

Safety first

You will need: colouring crayons, pencils or paints.

- Think about some of the dangers of electricity that you have talked about at school.
- Go out for a walk with your helper and look for pylons, sub-stations and railway lines near your home.
- Make a poster to warn people about the dangers of electricity.

Dear Helper,

Your child has been learning about situations in which electricity, if misused, can be very dangerous (including playing near pylons, using electrical appliances near water and overloading sockets). Encourage your child to recall these and add any others that they can think of, such as running over the lawnmower flex or drilling through electrical cables. On your walk, look for any examples of the dangers of electricity, and challenge your child to say why such situations are dangerous. (Because electric shocks can kill.)

Name:

What uses batteries?

- Find as many things at home as you can that use batteries.
- Can some of them use mains electricity as well?
- Fill in the table.

Picture and name of object	Battery type	Can also use mains ✓

Dear Helper,

This activity will help your child understand that electrical appliances generally get their electricity from one of two sources: the mains or batteries (although some devices can use either). Look around the house together, and discuss with your child where they think an object gets its energy from before filling in the table. When looking at objects, make sure that they are switched off and unplugged for safety. Make sure your child understands that they should never try to open a battery since it contains harmful chemicals.

Name:

Complete the circuit

- Look at the objects below.
- Draw in the components needed to complete the circuit so that it will work.
- Write the correct name of the component in the boxes.

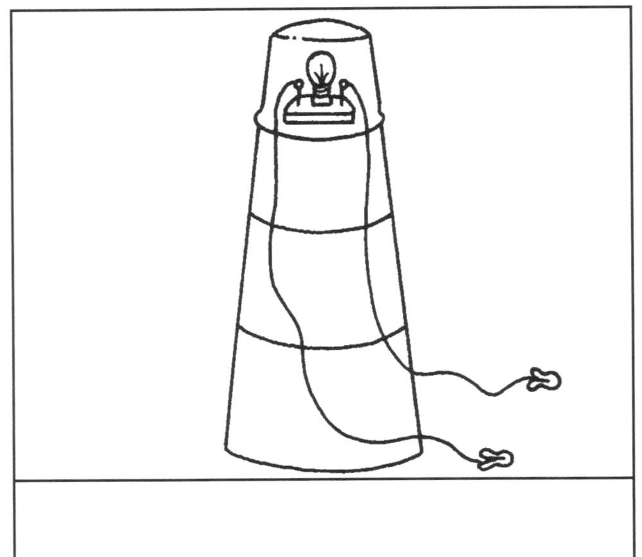

- These words may help you.

battery **bulb** **wire**

Dear Helper,

Your child has been learning that a complete circuit is needed to make a device work. Look at each picture with your child and help them to work out which component is missing. Help them to draw in what is missing and write the name of the component in the box.

Name:

UNIT 6 FORCES & MOTION · MAKING THINGS MOVE

Pull or push?

- Name the force that is being used in these pictures.
- Is it a pull or a push? Write **pull** or **push** below each picture.

- Colour the pictures once you've filled in all the words.

Dear Helper,

Your child has been learning about forces, including how forces cause things to move. You can help to reinforce this learning by talking about which force they are using when they perform everyday actions, in terms of simple pushes and pulls. Look at each of the pictures on the sheet and talk with your child about whether they think it shows a push or a pull – you might like to try the actions out if they are having difficulty deciding.

PHOTOCOPIABLE

Name:

Push, pull or twist?

- Think of as many things as you can that use stretching, squeezing, squashing, twisting and turning forces.
- Draw pictures of yourself doing them in the spaces below, and write the name of the force (push, pull, or twist) you are using underneath.

Dear Helper,

Help your child to think about and explain the forces they are using when performing a simple action that causes something to move or change shape. This will reinforce what they have learned at school about forces, and will help them to complete the sheet. For example, they could draw and label squeezing a sponge, turning (twisting) a tap or doorknob, stretching an elastic band around something, kneading (pushing) pastry or dough, and so on.

Name:

Forces wordsearch

- Find the forces words. (The words go across or down.)
- Cross each word off as you find it.

friction **slow down** **stop** **movement** **smooth** **surface** **rub** **rough**

A	R	F	R	I	C	T	I	O	N
F	Z	O	X	T	L	J	U	D	E
S	L	O	W	D	O	W	N	L	M
M	U	J	X	Q	D	Y	T	V	O
O	S	U	R	F	A	C	E	B	V
O	D	W	N	M	R	H	B	R	E
T	X	P	S	Z	O	D	R	E	M
H	S	T	O	P	U	Y	U	Z	E
A	V	G	J	Y	G	R	B	X	N
X	K	C	R	O	H	I	S	W	T

Which of these words describes the force that acts when two surfaces are rubbing against each other? ____________________

Dear Helper,

This activity will help reinforce the vocabulary about forces that your child has been learning in class. Challenge your child to create their own forces wordsearch for another member of the family to solve.

Name:

Speeding up, slowing down

- Look around your home for things that speed up, slow down or change direction.

Forces made these things		
speed up	**slow down**	**change direction**

- Choose one thing from each list and complete these sentences.

The ______________ speeded up because ______________

____

The ______________ slowed down because ______________

____

The ______________ changed direction because ______________

____

Dear Helper,

Your child is learning that forces can make things speed up, slow down or change direction. Look with them for everyday examples, such as a bicycle speeding up because the cyclist pushes harder on the pedals or slowing down because they have applied the brakes, or a sportsperson hitting a ball to change its direction. Talk with your child about what is happening and why.

Name:

Sinking bottles

You will need: a large empty plastic bottle with a top, an empty yoghurt pot, a bowl full of water (you could do this in the bath).

- Put your empty bottle (with the top on it) in the water. It should float. Push down on the bottle. Can you feel the water pushing up?
- Pour one yoghurt pot full of water into the bottle, replace the lid and try again. What happens to the bottle this time?
- Repeat this until the bottle sinks. How many containers full of water did it take to sink your bottle?
- Draw what your bottle looks like in the water in the bowls below.

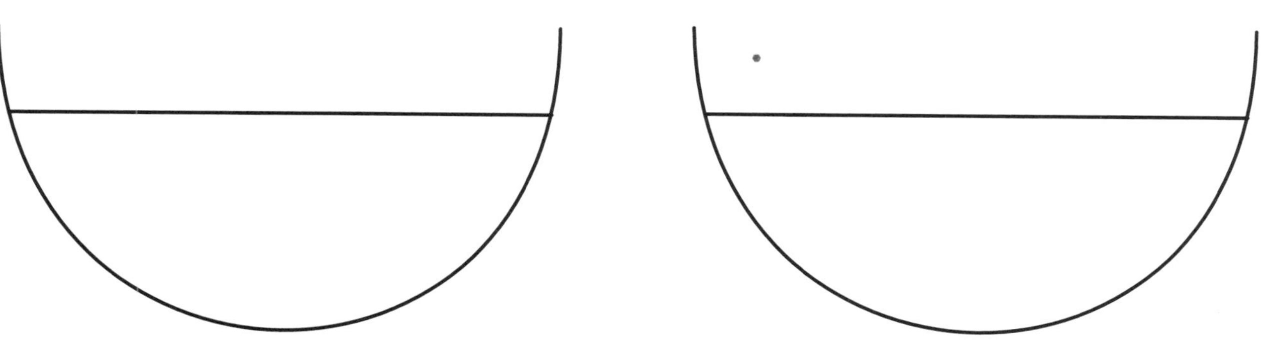

When the bottle is empty

When the bottle sinks

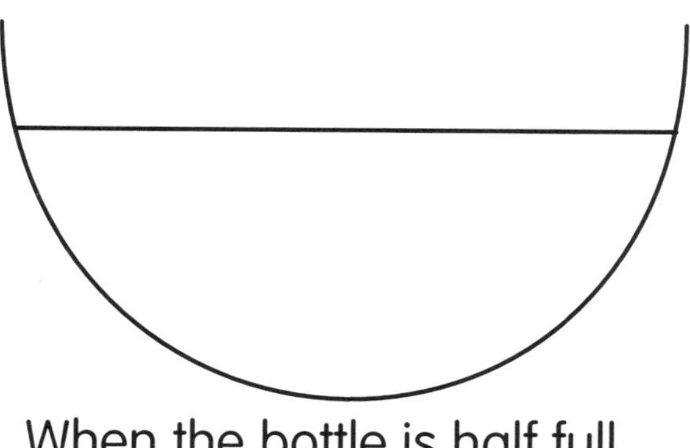

When the bottle is half full

Dear Helper,

You will need a full sink or a fairly deep bowl or bucket (or the bath) for this activity, as there needs to be enough water for the bottle to sink completely. Encourage your child to talk about what is happening as they do this activity. Help them to notice how the bottle slowly gets lower in the water and needs less of a push to make it sink as it is filled up. If you have scales, challenge your child to weigh the bottle to find out the weight of water it took to sink the bottle.

Name:

All lit up

- Look for sources of light around the home and note how they are used. Some may be used in more than one way.
- Draw pictures in the spaces below and write about what they are used for.

Dear Helper,

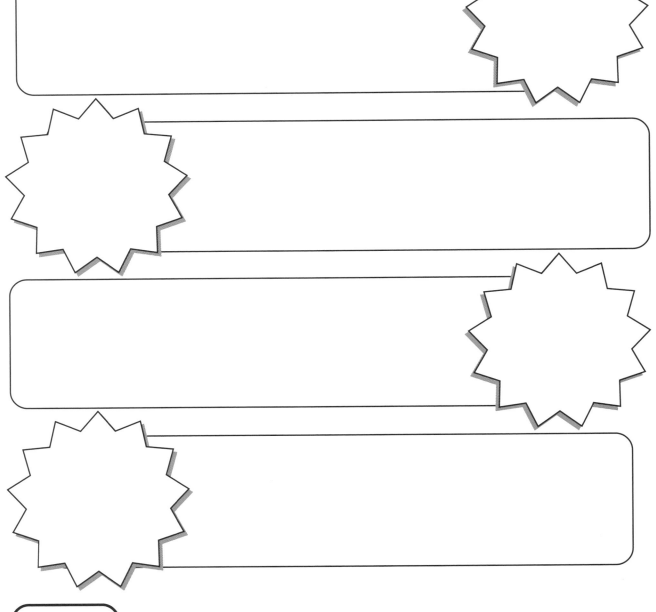

Help your child to look for light sources around the home, and talk about what they are used for. Encourage your child to write more than just *to see by*, and think of a specific use for the light (for example, a bedside lamp is used for reading in bed). This will help them understand that we use light sources in different ways. Talk about how sometimes we use light for decorative purposes. Challenge your child to find as many light sources as they can.

Name:

Shadows

- Use a table lamp or bright torch and a selection of objects to make shadows on the wall.
- Draw the shadows in the space below.

- Choose only objects that are opaque.

Dear Helper,

Make sure you supervise your child if you are using a table lamp, and that they do not move it themselves; a bright torch is best if you have one. Your child has been learning that shadows are formed because light cannot pass through some materials (these are called opaque materials). Help them to choose some opaque objects and to make shadows on the wall. (It is easier to see shadows on a plain wall, or you could put up a piece of white paper.) Challenge your child to make the sharpest shadow they can by moving the object nearer or further from the light source (you will get a sharper shadow as the object moves closer to the wall on which the shadow is cast).

Name:

Transparent, translucent, opaque

- Look around the house, and find some objects that are transparent, some that are translucent and some that are opaque.
- Draw the objects in the correct space below.

Transparent	Translucent	Opaque

Dear Helper,

Your child has been looking at the difference between objects that are transparent (see-through), translucent (let some light through) and opaque (let no light through). This activity will help to reinforce this understanding. Look around the house together and find several objects that fit into each category. Point out how you can see clearly through transparent objects, but you cannot see through opaque objects at all. Talk about how translucent objects let some light pass through them, but you cannot see things clearly. Challenge your child to think of different uses for each kind of material.

Name:

Solar energy

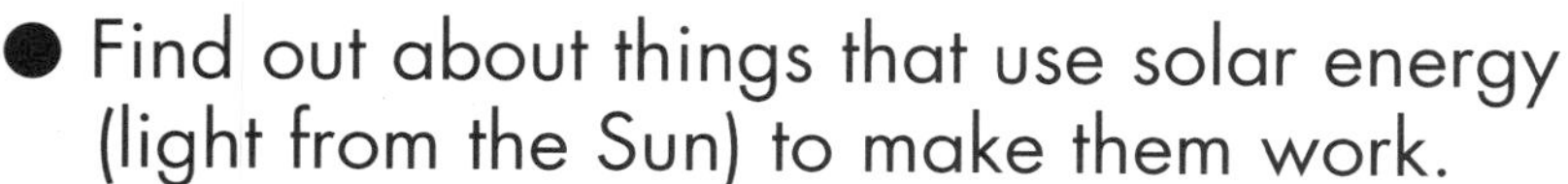

- Find out about things that use solar energy (light from the Sun) to make them work.
- Ask an adult, or use the library or the Internet to find information.
- Write or draw what you find in the space below.

Dear Helper,

This activity will help your child understand light as a source of energy. Help them find information from books, and to record what they find in the space above. Try to encourage them to record the information in their own words, rather than simply copying text. Some things that use solar energy to make them work include torches, fountains, calculators and garden lights. Newer buildings sometimes have solar panels to collect the Sun's energy and convert it to electricity for heating and so on. Talk to your child about some of the advantages of using solar energy. (It is free and does not cause pollution.)

Name:

Sounds at home

- Listen carefully to all the sounds you can hear at home in one evening. Make a list of what you hear.

- Choose one of the sounds that you heard during the evening and write about it. What kind of sound was it? What did it tell you? Was it a useful sound? Was it a pleasant sound?

Dear Helper,

Sound is all around us, although we may not pay attention to much of it. This activity will encourage your child to listen carefully to the sounds around them and to think about what they mean. As they make their list, talk about where the sounds they hear come from, and whether they are warning sounds, nice sounds, or useful in some other way. It may help your child to tell you what they want to write before they write it. Help them with any words they find difficult.

Name:

Warning sounds

- Play 'Sound I-spy', and record all the warning sounds you hear this week.
- Put a tick in the first column if you hear the sound, and another tick in the second column if you hear the sound more than once.

Outside	✔	✔
Ambulance		
Fire engine		
Police car		
Lorry reversing		
Car alarm		
Pelican crossing		
Car horn		
Train level crossing		
Burglar alarm		

At home	✔	✔
Alarm clock		
Doorbell		
Oven timer		
Burglar alarm		
Telephone		
Microwave		
Smoke alarm		

- Did you hear any others that were not on the lists? What were they?

Dear Helper,

Many sounds act as warnings, some alerting us to danger, and some reminding us that we need to do something (for example, answer the door or turn the oven off). Encourage your child to listen carefully to any sounds they hear over the course of a week, and to tell you what they think the sound means. Ask your child to tell you what they would do if they heard a sound warning them of danger.

Name:

Making sounds

- Make a range of instruments using objects found in the kitchen. Always ask permission first and do not use anything that might get broken. You could try using saucepan lids, metal trays and plastic washing-up bowls, with wooden spoons as beaters.
- See how many different sounds you can make with your instruments.
- Write a list of your instruments below and give each one a number.

What did you use?	Number
pan lid	*1*

- See if you and your helper can make up a tune. Use your number code to write the tune down so you can play it again.

Dear Helper,

This activity is quite noisy, but it will help your child to learn about how sounds are made. Try to join in with them, exploring the range of sounds that you can make using non-breakable kitchen equipment. Challenge your child to try to make a series of rhythms or tunes using their instruments, and see if they can write their sequences down in code, so that they can be repeated. If you have a tape recorder you might like to record your tunes so your child can share them with the rest of the class.

Name:

Sound puzzle

- Fill in the correct words to complete the crossword. Use the clues to help you.

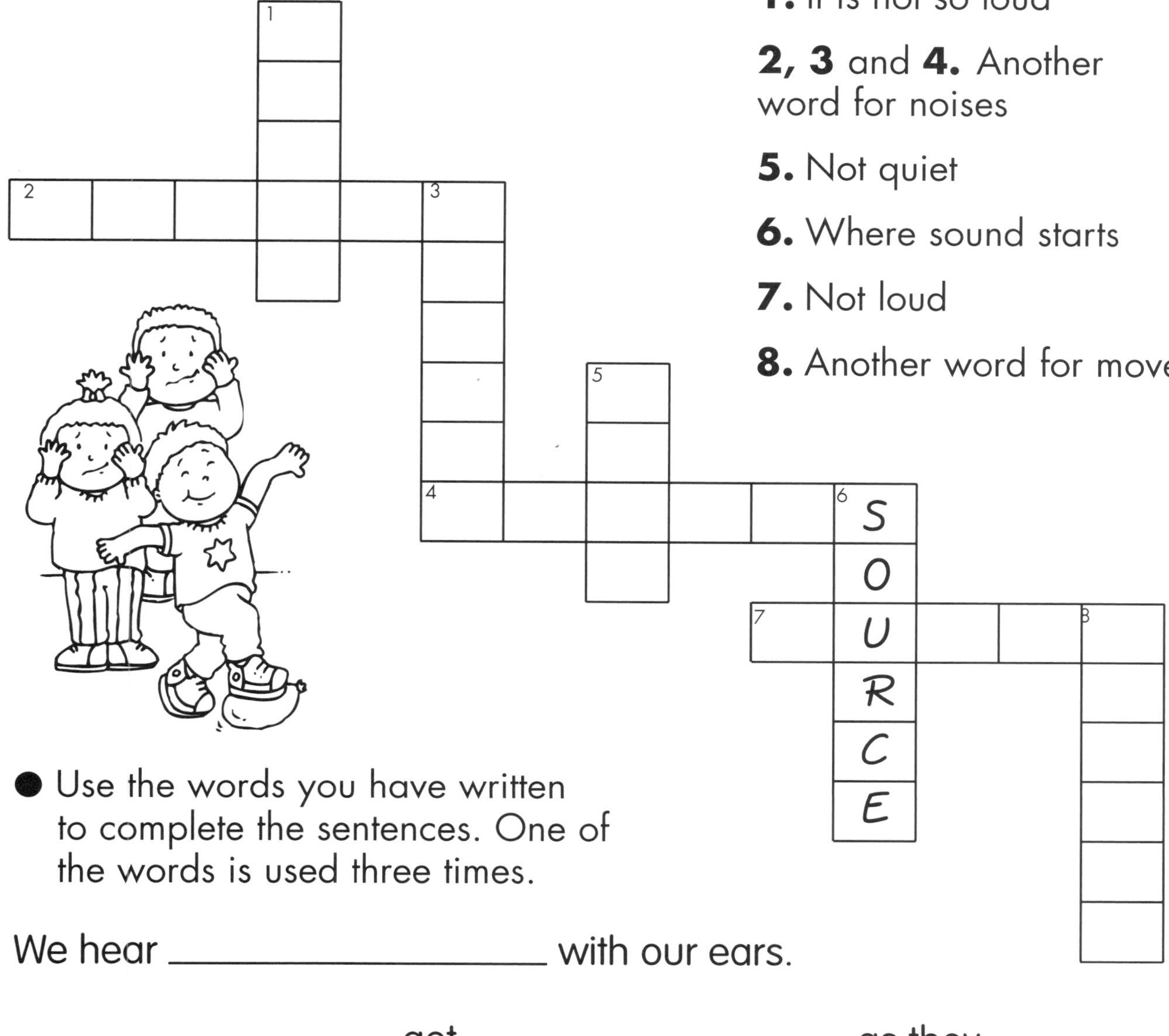

1. It is not so loud

2, 3 and **4.** Another word for noises

5. Not quiet

6. Where sound starts

7. Not loud

8. Another word for move

- Use the words you have written to complete the sentences. One of the words is used three times.

We hear ________________ with our ears.

________________ get ________________ as they

________________ away from the ________________.

________________ sounds travel further than

________________ ________________.

Dear Helper,

This crossword will help your child to recap on all the work they have been doing about sound in class. Fold the bottom of the sheet over so that they cannot see the answers as you do the crossword.

1. faint; 2, 3, and 4. sounds; 5. loud; 6. source; 7. quiet; 8. travel

Name:

Sun diary

- Choose a tree, lamppost or building near your home. Look at it each morning and evening and draw the object and its shadow.

- Look at the direction and size of the shadow.
- Was the shadow in the same place morning and evening?

- Can you explain what you found out?

Day	Morning	Evening
Monday		
Tuesday		
Wednesday		
Thursday		
Friday		
Saturday		
Sunday		

Dear Helper,

Encourage your child to make their observations at the same time, and from the same place, each day to notice that the Sun appears to move in the sky. If there are any days when you cannot see any shadows, encourage them to draw a cloud in the space to show that they made an observation but that the Sun was not visible and so there were no shadows. Help your child to write any sentence suggesting that the Sun appears to move across the sky in a regular way each day. Remind your child *never* to look directly at the Sun (even through sunglasses) as this can damage their eyes.

Name:

The Moon in space

- Find out as much as you can about the Moon and the people who have landed on it.
- Use books from home or the library, or use the Internet, to find the answers to these questions.

What is the Moon made of? ____________________

Why do we see the Moon? ____________________

____

____

When did people first land on the Moon? ____________________

How did they get there? ____________________

____

Why do people have to wear spacesuits on the Moon?

____

Why don't things grow on the Moon? ____________________

____

- Add anything else you find out about the Moon that you think is interesting on the back of this sheet.

Dear Helper,

Help your child to find information about the Moon in any books you have at home, or by visiting the local library. If you have access to the Internet, they may enjoy searching for information on the Web as well; this will help them to learn not only facts about the Moon but that information is available from many different sources and in many different formats. Make sure, though, that your child doesn't simply copy information straight from a website, and that they read it through to select the most relevant parts of any text they find. Challenge your child to find out how much they would weigh if they were on the Moon (it would be one-sixth of their weight on Earth, as the Moon's gravity is one-sixth that of the Earth).

Name:

Mapping the weather

- What kind of weather would you see in each season?
- Draw lines from the symbols to show what the weather might be like in each season.

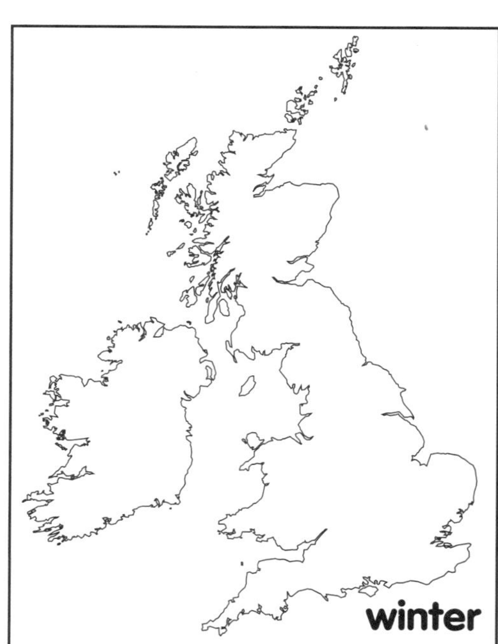

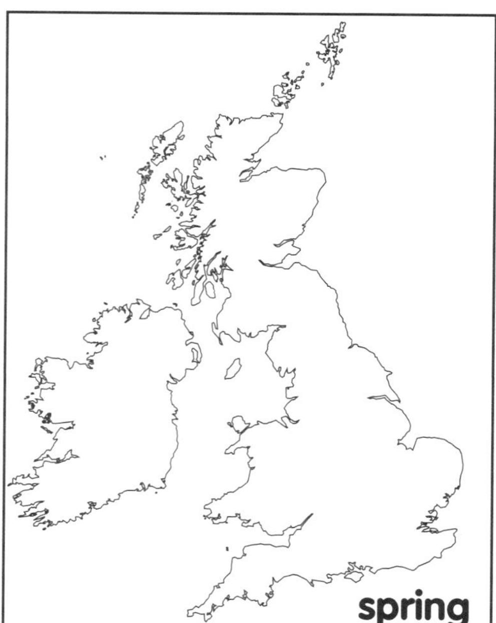

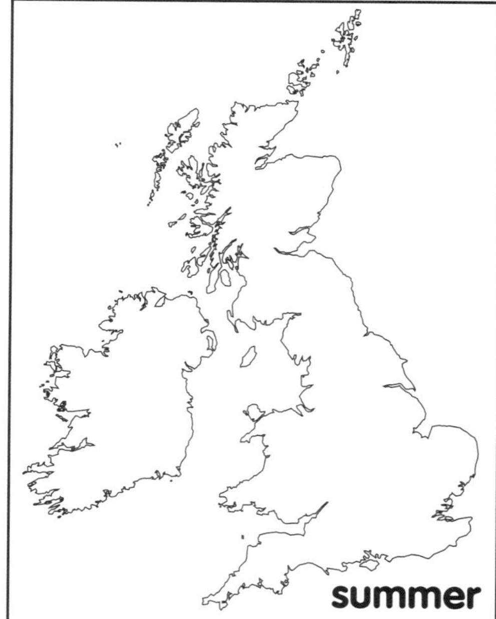

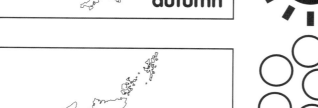

Dear Helper,

This activity will help your child understand that there are different weather patterns in different seasons. Watch the TV weather forecast together and look at the symbols used. Encourage them to notice which ones are used most frequently and to think about which season it is at the moment. Talk about the type of weather you might expect to see in a different season, and then help your child to stick the symbols onto the relevant maps on the sheet.